The Louvre and the Metropolitan Museum of Art: The History and Works of the Top Art Museums in the World

By Charles River Editors

The Louvre

D1377351

About Charles River Editors

Charles River Editors is a boutique digital publishing company, specializing in bringing history back to life with educational and engaging books on a wide range of topics. Keep up to date with our new and free offerings with this 5 second sign up on our weekly mailing list, and visit Our Kindle Author Page to see other recently published Kindle titles.

We make these books for you and always want to know our readers' opinions, so we encourage you to leave reviews and look forward to publishing new and exciting titles each week.

Introduction

A 1914 picture of the Met

"Keep good company - that is, go to the Louvre." - Paul Cezanne

"The Metropolitan Museum of Art is unsurpassed at presenting more than 50 centuries of work. I go there constantly, seeing things over and over, better than I've ever seen them before." - Jerry Saltz

The Louvre: The very name conjures up scenes of art and elegance, and of long halls filled with beauty and people strolling through them whispering quietly among themselves about the glories they are witnessing. Even those who have never been to the Louvre know some of its most prized possessions, from ancient statues to Leonardo Da Vinci's "Mona Lisa". As the world's largest museum, the Louvre is unquestionably the cultural highpoint of Paris, a city that has long been considered the cultural center of Europe.

However, life is rarely as simple as one imagines, and the life of the Louvre is no different. While just about everyone is familiar with its history as an art museum, the Louvre's history goes back over 800 years, and it used to have far different purposes, both as a medieval fortress and a palatial residence for French kings. The Louvre bore witness to mass murder during the French Revolution, and there have been countless accusations of theft and other questionable actions since its opening.

Furthermore, the museum is also a classic example of beating one's swords into ploughshares, for it has been largely stocked through the conquests of war. Its first collection was put on display by a king who wanted to share his personal art collection with his subjects. Following the French Revolution, the Louvre became a place of ascetic refuge, where those burdened by daily life could go, often at no cost, and visit some of the most beautiful pieces of art in the world. While the power hungry Napoleon made war across the continent, he was also always on the lookout for beautiful and interesting items to send home to his people. Later, when rioters attempted to burn the building down, the museum portion of the palace survived, almost by miracle, and when the Nazis occupied Paris, they found that most of the items of value had been safely sent away. Ironically, when World War II was over, the museum became a safehouse for items stolen by the Germans from around the world, and a conduit to get the pieces back to their rightful owners. Even now, in the 21st century, the museum is serving as a bridge to peace and understanding; its latest gallery was designed to showcase Islamic art in the hope of bringing together people from different cultures. This is, to say the least, quite a change of pace for a fortress originally intended to fight off invaders.

Americans are rightfully proud of much of their heritage, especially as it relates to the ideas of democracy and government. The country has spread its ideals throughout the world and rose, in just two short centuries, to a place of global leadership. However, when it comes to art and culture, there's never been any doubt how young the nation is, especially compared to much older nations across the Atlantic. The Metropolitan Museum of Art was created to assuage some of that, and to show the world that America could hold its own with the leading galleries of the rest of the world.

From the beginning, the Met has been unique, because unlike many European museums, the support for the sprawling New York City museum came from modern tycoons and philanthropists, instead of old families with wealth and land. Like the rest of the city, the museum grew quickly, as the millionaires of New York and other cities around the nation vied to see who could donate the most paintings or objects of art. Having one's work in the Met, or contributing to it, became something of a status symbol, a way to demonstrate prestige and importance. Having one's name on a gallery wall or a wing of the always expanding museum could cement a legacy.

At the same time, the Met has always been a place that anyone could visit. Its very charter insisted that patrons be welcomed and educated by what they saw during their visits, a goal the museum has kept in focus for nearly 150 years. And while many European museums cater primarily to tourists, the Met remains something of a hometown treasure for New York City, focusing much of its attention on recognizing and balancing the city's cultural diversity with the needs of its patrons of all ages and socioeconomic backgrounds.

The Louvre and the Metropolitan Museum of Art: The History and Works of the Top Art Museums in the World chronicles the remarkable history of both museums and highlights some of their most important pieces. Along with pictures depicting important people, places, and events, you will learn about the Met and the Louvre like never before.

The Origins of the Louvre

Though may be hard to imagine today, the Louvre was not originally a place of tranquility and beauty but a spot for war. King Philip II of France built Louvre Palace in the mid-12th century to house him and his men during the still frequent Viking attacks, and it is even possible that some of the earliest parts of the building, which can now only be seen in the depths of the museum's ancient crypt, date back even earlier. Author M. Vitet revealed, "According to some, the Louvre was founded by Childebert; according to others, by Louis Le Gros. It was either a place from which to hunt the wolf, a' louveterie' (Jupara), or, according to another view, a fortress commanding the river in front of the city. It seems probable that before the time of Philip Augustus there was a fortified castle where now stands the Louvre, and that this king simply altered it, and indeed reconstructed it, but was not its founder…The historians of the time speak frequently of the great tower built in 1204 by this prince, to which the name of New Tower was given; an evident sign of the existence of some other more ancient tower. It was not in any case until 1204 that, for the first time, the name of Louvre was officially pronounced. Until then the field is open to conjectures."

A medieval portrait of the coronation of King Philip
II

The seal of King Philip II

Pictures of the medieval foundations of the Louvre by

Pierre-Emmanuel Malissin and Frédéric Valdes

According to author Henry Edwards, writing in the 19th century, "The castle was at that time in the form of a large square, in the midst of which was a big tower, with its own independent system of defense. The tower was 144 feet in circumference, and 96 feet in height. Its walls were 13 feet thick near the basement, and 12 feet in the upper part. A gallery at the top put it in communication with the buildings of the first enclosure, and it served at once as treasury and as prison."

C.J. Dub's picture of part of the wall constructed by Philip II

During its first two centuries of existence, the Louvre

served as a pet project for a number of kings as they changed its configuration, pulled down some structures, built new ones, and pulled down still others. The one constant was that French forces remained able to retire behind its mighty walls to defend themselves from their enemies. Edwards noted, "Louis IX…arranged in the west wing of the Louvre a large hall, which was long known as the Chamber of St. Louis. Charles V…enlarged and embellished the Louvre. He added to it another storey, and did all in his power to change what had hitherto been a purely military building into a convenient and agreeable place of abode. The architecture of the building, originally constructed for use, not show, was in many respects improved, and the gates were surmounted with ornaments and pieces of sculpture."

A medieval statue of Louis IX

Napoleon Veir's picture of a statue of Charles V of France

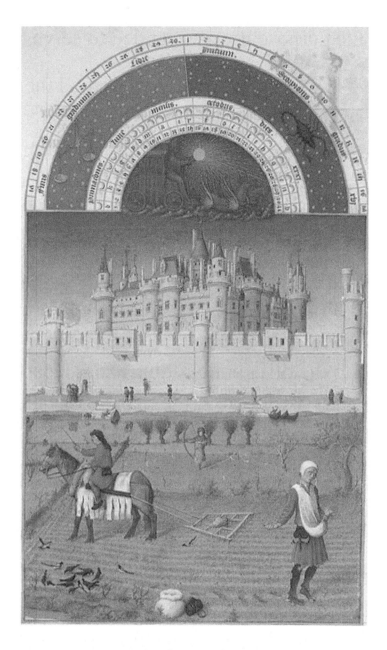

A contemporary depiction of the Louvre at the time of Charles V's reign

Furthermore, the reception rooms were away from the river, and looked out upon a street long since disappeared, called La Rue Froidmanteaux. The apartments of the king and queen looked out upon the river. Each of the towers was designated by a particular name, according to its history or the purpose it was intended to serve.

In the mid-14th Century, Charles V settled there, making the palace his permanent home. He also created its first major collection, establishing a library containing more than 1,200 books, both ancient and contemporary. These would become the first books of the National Library. Charles also "added to the Louvre a number of buildings for tradespeople and domestics, whose services had to be dispensed with when the Louvre was purely a military building. Such names as pantry, pastry, saucery, butlery, were given to the different buildings and departments by the bakers, the pastry-cooks, the makers of sauces, and the keepers of the wine."

At this time, the palace did not enclose much land, but what was there was well cultivated and quite beautiful. However, Charles VI, feeling the need for more security than beauty, tore out the gardens on the river side of the palace and replaced them with stronger fortifications against any potential enemy attacking from the water.

Shifting Focus

In1546, Francis I decided to update the castle, recreating it in the then popular French Renaissance style. Architects Arthur Vye-Parminter and Charles Saunier recorded, "He began in 1527 by demolishing the old tower of Philippe Auguste which gave to the old building the aspect of a prison…for some time an army of work men were employed in decorating the old building as splendidly as possible; the walls were covered with paintings and tapestries, and the salient portions of the building, even to the weather-cocks, were decorated and gilded, and a number of the old towers pulled down to make room for the lists of a tournament."

Unfortunately, Francis seems to have had his eye on the wrong prize, as the article indicated: "But all this was of little avail, the old palace was falling to pieces and threatened ruin on all sides, so Francois I…after having spent a large sum of money in repairs, decided to demolish the building…and con struct a new palace after the fashion and the new style which was growing in France under Italian influence…According to the plan of Pierre Lescot the new palace was to occupy the perimeter of the old building and be composed of four facades with a pavilion at each angle. A portion of the foundations of the fortress of Philippe Auguste was utilised and the western wing of the present building rests on these old foundations. … At the death of Francois I, in 1547, very little of the proposed work had been completed, and it was only at the end of Henri II. that the facade on the western side, the angle pavilion called Pavillon du Roi, and a portion of the facade on the river side were terminated."

A 15th century depiction of the Louvre

Francis I

More important than the work that Francis did on the buildings, however, were his efforts to acquire beautiful art for his palace. Without a doubt, his most important purchase came from Italy, in the form of Leonardo da Vinci's "Mona Lisa".

Around early 1503, Leonardo began work in earnest on his most famous painting, which is likely a portrait of Lisa di Anto Maria di Noldo Gherardini, who had married Francesco di Bartolommeo de Zenobi del Giocondo in 1495. From her husband's name, Giocondo, she, and later her well-known portrait, gained the nickname La Joconde. The portrait may have been started as early as 1501, prior to Leonardo's work with Cesare Borgia or as late as 1505. While the portrait's subject was in all probability a Florentine noble woman, she never received the painting.

The "Mona Lisa"

A portrait of Leonardo

The "Mona Lisa" shows the serene woman in front of a rather harsh landscape, but in contrast to the landscape behind her, her face is quite delicate. While the painting has been poorly restored several times over the centuries, it likely was even finer than it appears today. Musicians entertained her while she sat for the portrait, providing the well-known "Mona Lisa" "smile". Soft shadows enhance the delicate tones of her skin.

The artistry of the "Mona Lisa" is impressive, but its unusual features have helped it endure as one of the most intriguing works of art in history. For that reason, there has long been speculation and rumor over just about every aspect of the "Mona Lisa". While most believe the "Mona Lisa" is Lisa del Giocondo, a lack of definitive proof has long led others to speculate that "Mona Lisa" was Leonardo's mother Caterina drawn from memory, or even a self-portrait of Leonardo himself. Other aspects of the painting have long been questioned, including whether the surviving work is the original, and why Leonardo made it. The landscape in back of the "Mona Lisa" was also a novel effect, leading others to wonder how and why Leonardo drew it like that.

Of course, the most interesting aspect of the painting is the facial expression of the "Mona Lisa", and for centuries people have argued over how Leonardo accomplished her enigmatic smile, or if it's even a smile at all. It is perhaps the most heavily analyzed aspect of any art in history, to an almost ridiculous extent. For example, scientific experiments about human vision have been used to explain why people characterize the nature of the smile differently, while one Harvard Professor has asserted that the nature of the smile changes based on whether a viewer looks at "Mona Lisa"'s eyes or looks at the painting from a distance.

Years after making the "Mona Lisa", Leonardo carried the painting with him to France, bequeathing it to his close acquaintance Salai upon his death, but eventually it was purchased by King Francis I and remained in the possession of the French royal family until the French Revolution. Art historian Cécile Scailliérez explains of the painting, "The "Mona Lisa" is the earliest Italian portrait to focus so closely on the sitter in a half-length portrait. The painting is generous enough in its dimensions to include the arms and hands without them touching the frame. The portrait is painted to a realistic scale in the highly structured space where it has the fullness of volume of a sculpture in the round. The figure is shown in half-length, from the head to the waist, sitting in a chair whose arm is resting on balusters…The "Mona Lisa"'s famous smile represents the sitter…. It is a visual representation of the idea of happiness suggested by the word "gioconda" in Italian. Leonardo made this notion of happiness the central motif of the portrait: it is this notion which makes the work such an ideal. The nature of the landscape also plays a role. The middle distance, on the same level as the sitter's chest, is in warm colors."

16th century engravings of the Louvre's façade

Francis and his successors may have valued art, but the famous "Sun King," Louis XIV, valued comfort and the ability to be near the center of things. To this end, he chose in 1682 to move his official residence to Versailles, leaving the Louvre available for artists to come and stay while studying and working. This was considered very stylish in late 17th century and 18th century, and by 1746, there was a move afoot to create a public gallery in Paris for the care and display of the nation's important art pieces. Art critic Etienne La Font of Saint-Yenne complained in *Dialogue du Grand Colbert*, "You doubtless remember, O Grand Minister, the immense and precious collection of pictures which you induced Louis XIV to have Italy and other foreign countries taken away with considerable expense to furnish worthily his palaces. You think that these riches are exposed to the admiration and joy of the French to possess such rare treasures, or to the curiosity of foreigners, or, finally, to the study and emulation of our school?" Answering his own question, he wrote, "Know, O Grand Colbert, that these fine works have not seen the light, and that they have passed from the honorable places which they occupied in the cabinets of their possessors to an obscure prison at Versailles, where they perish for more than ever fifty years."

The following year, Saint-Yenne published *Reflections on some Causes of the Present State of Painting in France, with an examination of the principal works exhibited at the Louvre, this month of August, 1746.* In it, he insisted, "The means which I propose for the most prompt and at the same time the most efficacious advantage for a durable re-establishment of painting, would be to choose in this palace, or somewhere, a place proper to place the chief…work of the greatest masters of Europe, and of an infinite price, which compose the cabinet of His Majesty's paintings, heaped up today, and buried in little rooms ill-lighted and hidden in the city of Versailles, or indifferent to the curiosity of foreigners by the impossibility of seeing them…Such would be the gallery which has just been proposed, built expressly in the Louvre, where all immense and unknown riches would be ranked in a fine order, and maintained in the best condition by an intelligent artist charged with watching carefully their perfect preservation…"

The Louvre in the late 17th century

Veüe et Perspectiue de la Galerie du Louure, dans laquelle sont les
Portraits des Roys des Reynes et des plus Illustres du Royaume.

The Louvre's Petite Galerie in the 17th century

On October 14, 1750, King Louis XV agreed to open
part of the Luxembourg Palace to the public. Visitors
could wander the halls of the Galerie royale de
peinture on Wednesdays and Saturdays and view some 96
pieces owned by the crown, including *Charity* by Andrea
del Sarto. According to the National Gallery of Art in the
United States, where that piece is currently on display,
"The theological virtue of Charity is traditionally
represented by a woman with several small children, one
of whom she is shown nursing. Here, those figures appear
hard and solid amidst a smoky, undefined setting. Sharp
colors, like the pink and turquoise of the garments or the
burnt orange and purple stripes of the tablecloth, heighten

this contrast of tangible form and indeterminate space. It is, above all, in the ideal grace of slowly revolving poses that the real expressive force of the picture is conveyed…Andrea d'Agnolo was called 'del Sarto' from his father's trade as a tailor. He had a successful and productive career in Florence and was particularly celebrated for the beauty and originality of his color. Sarto worked briefly at the court of Francis I at Fontainebleau in 1518. This Charity, probably painted shortly before the artist's death, was also commissioned for the French king."

Louis XV

As it turned out, the museum at Luxemburg Palace was

short lived; in 1780, the crown took back the building, and eight years later, the king gave it to the Count of Provence, Louis XVIII, for his home. However, the idea of a national art museum was not forgotten, and with the blessing of Louis XVI, the Comte d'Angiviller converted the Grande Galerie of the Louvre into a new royal museum.

Louis XVI

While many supported this proposition, the court was already in disarray and those in power could never agree on how the museum would be organized. Ironically, it would be the revolutionaries who ruled the country during the chaos of the French Revolution who ultimately helped convert the Louvre into a functioning museum that could be open to the public.

The Napoleonic Era

Napoleon

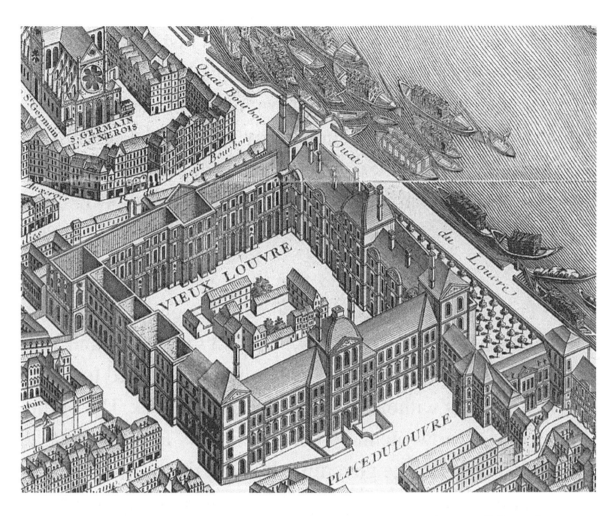

A map depicting the Louvre during the reign of Louis XVI

On May 26, 1791, the Legislative Assembly declared, "The Louvre and the Tuileries combined shall be the national palace, as such to serve as the king's residence and as a place for bringing together monuments of all the sciences and arts as well as the leading public educational establishments." However, the Louvre did not house the king for long, as King Louis XVI was imprisoned the following year and executed in January 1793. With that, his vast art collection became public property.

Aware that a period of mob rule was just a dangerous to art as it was to human life, the National Assembly demanded that steps be made right away to safely house the irreplaceable collection. They appointed a commission to gather together the various pieces of art scattered throughout the royal residences in France and bring them to Paris, where they could be properly stored and cared for.

Thanks to all these efforts, the Louvre opened as a public museum on August 10, 1793 with 537 paintings and 184 other pieces of artwork. The public was allowed to tour the exhibits without charge three days a week. Historian Bette Oliver wrote in 2007, "As early as January 1794, the Conservatoire, the governing body of the Louvre, had expanded its mission beyond the collection of French works: The national museums mission, other than instructing those who came to view or to study the collections, included saving the art treasures already confiscated as well as those soon to be arriving from foreign conquests. The revolutionary government perceived the Muséum Français as a place where much of the world's great art could be protected, restored, and displayed in the best possible manner..."

There was a problem with the Louvre's holdings from the very beginning, however, one that has plagued it for its entire history: much of its prized collection had been stolen, or at the very least taken from its owners under duress. Even within the first collection, a quarter of the pieces came from those emigrating to other countries and the Catholic Church. The rest of the art came from the crown, and while many among the public considered that art the property of the people, the works' former owners were by this time dead or awaiting execution by the same people who were organizing the exhibits.

Beginning in 1794, French armies under Napoleon and others would bring back pieces plundered from all over the world. For example, one work brought to France was *Laocoon and His Sons*, an ancient sculpture praised by Pliny the Elder as being one "of several works of very great excellence…the Laocoön, for example, in the palace of the Emperor Titus, a work that may be looked upon as preferable to any other production of the art of painting or of [bronze] statuary. It is sculptured from a single block, both the main figure as well as the children, and the serpents with their marvellous folds. This group was made in concert by three most eminent artists, Agesander, Polydorus, and Athenodorus, natives of Rhodes."

Livio Andronico's picture of the sculpture

   The Louvre's establishment as an art museum came during a time of unrest and revolution, and its early exhibits reflected this chaos. As he sought to dominate Europe, Napoleon was anxious to have France considered first in all aspects of culture, wealth, and power, and to this end one of the first acts of his reign was to order a wing on the north side of the building to be built. Later named the Grande Galerie, he was able to fill it with items he took during his military campaigns. As author Edward Alexander observed: "The pictures were hung frame to frame from floor to ceiling by schools but within the schools according to the old miscellaneous principle; there were no labels, so that the museum was a confusing labyrinth for the untutored visitor. The hall was lighted by windows from two sides, and on bright days the pictures were exposed to too much sunlight…Fortunately, Hubert Robert, former keeper of the royal collection, was respected in the new order and managed to maintain tolerable standards of housekeeping and conservation. The Louvre was in such bad structural condition that it had to be closed in May 1796, not to open fully again until July 14, 1801. The Grand Galerie was then more rationally arranged on a chronological principle; a few years later, marble columns and statues divided the long vista of the gallery, and the overhead lighting was obtained."

One item taken back to France from abroad was Apollo Belvedere, of which art historian Kenneth Clark wrote, "For four hundred years after it was discovered the Apollo was the most admired piece of sculpture in the world. It was Napoleon's greatest boast to have looted it from the Vatican." It was later featured on the logo for the Apollo XVII moon landing.

Livio Andronico's picture of the Apollo Belvedere

Napoleon did not just want the art for its own sake, nor was he the only one interested in these acquisitions. The French Director saw France as the liberator of pieces that, in his all-important opinion, were not being properly cared for or appreciated by their own governments. Thus, they were happy to dispatch scientists and art experts to join Napoleon's forces on their campaigns, and after the smoke of battle cleared, they would go in, catalogue, and often pack up priceless art pieces for shipment back to France.

At the same time, Napoleon took a personal interest not only in filling the museum but also in how the items he brought back were displayed. He returned from Egypt in 1801, just as the museum was preparing to reopen, and took it upon himself to appoint Dominique Vivant Denon as the organization's first director. Denon had traveled with Napoleon through Egypt and therefore was able to offer an excellent record of some of their more famous acquisitions: "We came afterwards to the obelisk, named Cleopatra's needle: another obelisk thrown down at its side, indicates that both of them formerly decorated one of the entrances of the palace of the Ptolomies, the ruins of which are still to be seen at some distance from thence. An inspection into the present state of these obelisks, and the fissures which existed at the time even when they were fixed on this spot, prove that they were merely fragments at that period, and that they had been brought from Memphis, or from upper Egypt…They might be conveyed to France without difficulty, and would there become a trophy of conquest, and a very characteristic one, as they are in themselves a monument, and as the hieroglyphics with which they are covered render them preferable to Pompey's pillar, which is merely a column, somewhat larger, indeed, than is everywhere to be found…On digging since round the base of this obelisk, it has been found that it was placed on a tablet of hard stone. The pedestals which have always been added in Europe to this species of monument, are an ornament by which its character is changed." Under Denon's direction, the Louvre became known as the "Musée Napoléon."

Denon

Napoleon did not always take what he wanted outright;

sometimes he bargained for it. As a result of the Treaty of Campo Formio, the defeated Italian cities promised to contribute pieces of art as part of several "parades of booty" that Napoleon planned for his return to Paris. After the pieces were shown throughout the city, he placed them in the Louvre for display.

Napoleon had no scruples about looting churches and other religious sites either. While in Rome, he took a number of items from Saint Peter's Basilica, and thanks to the Treaty of Tolentino, the French took possession of the Nile and Tiber, two famous statues that had once belonged to the Vatican. The Nile was later returned, but the Tiber remains at the Louvre today.

The Tiber

By this time, the Louvre had developed a reputation

across Rueope for both the quality and quantity of its holdings. Writing in 1814, Sir Archibald Alison claimed, "For an attempt of this kind, the Louvre presents singular advantages, from the unparalleled collection of paintings of every school and description which are there to be met with, and the facility with which you can there trace the progress of the art from its first beginning to the period of its greatest perfection…And it is in this view that the collection of these works into one museum, however much to be deplored as the work of unprincipled ambition, and however much it may have diminished the impression which particular objects, from the influence of association, produced in their native place, is yet calculated to produce the greatest of all improvements in the progress of the art…by divesting particular schools and particular works of the unbounded influence which the effect of early association, or the prejudices of national feeling, have given them in their original situation, and placing them where their real nature is to be judged of by a more extended circle, and subjected to the examination of more impartial sentiments."

Alison

Modern History

Napoleon's reign was dramatic but relatively short-lived, and when he fell from power, many nations hoped that they would be able to reacquire the items he had taken. However, the men running the Louvre were determine to keep as much of their collection intact as possible, to the point that when nations sent inspectors to look for the missing pieces, the French moved the items out of the museum and into private homes. Many of the more determined countries refused to give up and eventually appealed to the British and their allies who had defeated the French for help. The victors were able to see many of the items returned, but the Louvre still retained more than its fair share of the treasures. In 1815, Lord Castlereagh wrote, "The spoliation of the Louvre is begun. The King of the Netherlands is hard at work; Austria begins immediately; and I believe the three Powers—that is Austria, Prussia, and Great Britain—if called upon by the Pope's Commissioner, Canova, will unite to enable him to remove his master's property. The Emperor of Russia will not, I hope, take any further part in opposition to the sentiments of the Allies. The French, of all parties, are very sore, and they were foolish enough, at Madame de Duras' the other night, to resent it to the Duke of Wellington in the most pointed manner; but we are going straight forward."

Lord Castlereagh

   After the Bourbon Restoration in the wake of the
Napoleonic Era, Louis XVIII made it his business to add a
number of new items to the museum's collection.
Between him and his successor, Charles X, they spent
more than 700,000 francs on new pieces for the Louvre.
Much of that money was spent forming a Department of
Egyptian Antiquities. The curator, Jean-François
Champollion, had devoted his life to the study of Egyptian
antiquities, specifically the language of Ancient Egypt. In
1806 he had written, "I want to conduct deep continuing
studies into this ancient nation. The enthusiasm which the
descriptions of their enormous monuments ignited in me,

the admiration which their power and knowledge filled me with, will grow with the new things that I will acquire. Of all the peoples that I love the most, I will confess that no one equals the Egyptians in my heart."

Louis XVIII

Champollion

Under Champollion's supervision, the museum acquired more than 7,000 new pieces of Egyptian art, most of them coming from several large private collections. Still, while the museum's collection was growing, its facilities were deteriorating, and by the time the French Second Republic took hold in 1848, the Louvre was in sorry shape indeed.

Fortunately, the new regime financed much-needed repairs and authorized the construction of several new galleries, including the the Salon Carré, the Galerie d'Apollon, and the Grande Galérie. In 1857, the *London*

Morning News reported, "By completing the union of the Louvre and the Tuileries, Napoleon III has identified his name with those of Francis I, Henry II, and the other Sovereigns of France who have contributed to the erection or enlargement of what is now the most extensive and most beautiful palace in the world…Fronting the Rue Rivoli, which is also of recent origin, the Tuileries and the Louvre, including their gardens, are now continuous from the Place de la Concorde to the Place-St. Germain L'Auxerrois. The new constructions necessary to unite the two palaces into one consist in a wing to the right and another to the left of the façade of the old Louvre, with a court open between them.… [I]t faces the old Louvre on one side, and the Arc du Triumphe du Carrousel on the other…Two gardens have been already made in the centre of this square.… Trees, fountains, and Iamps will be of course employed to add to the beauty of these enclosures, and the façade of the old Louvre on the side of the new Place will be ornamented in harmony with the two wings. In addition to these wings a block of building presenting a very handsome front to the Rue Rivoli has been erected."

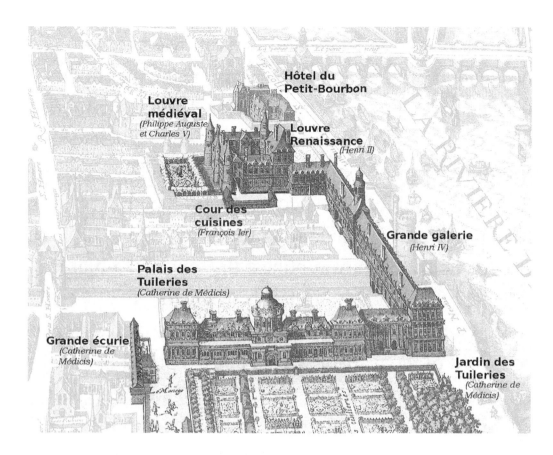

A layout of the grounds

In 1861, Napoleon III bought nearly 12,000 additional works for the museum, many of them from the famed Campana collection. Writing of the collection some years earlier, art critic Blewett said, "The specimens consist for the most part of gold ornaments, earrings in the form of genii, necklaces of scarabæi, filigree brooches, bracelets, neck chains, torques, chapelets in form of foliage &c.; the head of the horned Bacchus, and a gold fibula with an Etruscan inscription, equal, if they do not surpass, the finest productions of Trichinopoly or Genoa…One of the most remarkable objects in this collection is a superb Scarabæus in sardonyx, representing Cadmus destroying the Dragon. The collection of Etruscan vases is also very fine, several presenting historical scenes, with Greek and Etruscan inscriptions. The Cabinet of Bronzes comprises a fine series of Etruscan and Roman objects: 2 beautiful tripods, a mirror of extraordinary beauty and size, and a cinerary urn of most rare occurrence in metal; it was found near Perugia, containing the ashes of the dead, with a golden necklace, now amongst the jewelry; a bier of bronze, with the bottom in latticework, like that in the Museo Gregoriano, with the helmet, breastplate, greaves and sword of the warrior whose body reposed upon it….There are several fine specimens of Etruscan helmets, with delicate wreaths of gold foliage placed upon them. The collection of glass and enamels is most interesting, consisting of elegant tazze of blue, white and yellow glass mounted on filigree stands precisely as they were taken from the tombs. The series of Etruscan vases, not only from Etruria proper, but from Magna Grecia, is rich and extensive."

Napoleon III

The French economy continued to thrive during the years that followed, and as it grew, so did the Louvre's collections. By 1870, there were 20,000 new items in the museum. However, the good times would not last much longer, because in 1871 Paris suffered a major blow when socialists rampaged through the city, looting the Louvre and other famous structures. The fighting reached its height in late May, and the *London Week News* reported about the damage: "On Wednesday, May 24, the Louvre, the Tuileries, the Palace of the Legion of Honour, the Palace of the Council of State, and several other public buildings of Paris were in flames. By three o'clock in the afternoon the Tuileries was entirely burnt down, and there was but little hope of saving the Louvre. The Versailles Fire Brigade was despatched to Paris with all haste, M. Thiers himself accompanying it to direct its operations. This horrible deed, which was accomplished by the use of petroleum, the fumes from the burning oil filling the air, was the work of the insurgents."

One reporter, working for *The Times*, wrote, "I have just returned from witnessing one of the saddest sights that has occurred in the world's history. I have been for some hours in the magnificent city, which flames and bombshells are fast reducing to a huge and shapeless ruin. Its architectural glories are rapidly passing; away in smoke and flame…and amid a roar of cannon, a screaming of mitrailleuses, a bursting of projectiles, and a horrid rattle of musketry from different quarters which are appalling…Such of the great buildings as the spreading conflagration has not reached stand in the clearest, relief as they are seen for probably the last time; but in a dozen spots…sheets of flame and awful volumes of smoke rise to the sky and positively obscure the light of the sun." Finally, "No one doubts that the Palais de Justice is sharing, the fate of the Tuileries and the Louvre. … The

Louvre is not yet wholly gone, and perhaps the fire will not reach all its courts. … Not an instant passes without an explosion. Stones and timber and iron are flying high into the air, and falling to the earth with horrible crashes. The very trees are on fire. They are crackling, and their leaves and branches are like tinder."

Amazingly, while much of the palace burned, the museum itself survived unscathed.

A depiction of the damage done to the Tuileries

Following the fire, the Louvre, and much of France, enjoyed a period of relative peace, but in 1911 it suffered a shocking loss when, on the night of August 21, the

"Mona Lisa" was stolen. The painting remained lost for two years until, in the fall of 1913, Vincenzo Peruggia, an Italian nationalist who had worked at the Louvre, was caught trying to sell the painting to the Uffizi Gallery in Florence. Peruggia maintained that he had only stolen the famed art because he wanted to see it returned to its original home in Italy. The Louvre got the painting back, and Peruggia got a light sentence of only six months for his crime.

Peruggia

The museum continued to add items to its collection, albeit on a smaller scale, until World War I broke out in 1914. On September 12, barely a month after the war began, a newspaper reported some of the measures taken by the Louvre to protect its art: "The famous statue of Venus de Milo once more lies buried in the ground, this time in a secret grave, and the priceless paintings in the world-famed Louvre are screened with iron and steel in order to protect them from the German bombardment of Paris which seemed imminent several weeks ago, according to stories related by tourists who returned here today from the French capital…The statue…was removed from its pedestal when the Germans' approach was announced, carefully packed in straw and then placed underground in an iron-bound box. The location of the 'interment' being known only to the officials of the Louvre. Of course, it was impossible to hide the paintings in a similar manner and out of the question to attempt the removal all of them to Bordeaux , so the iron and steel screens were decided upon as the next best plan for their protection and preservation. …many other pieces of statuary and priceless bric-a-brac and ornaments which are numbered among the Louvre treasures were buried in secret graves."

Livio Andronico's picture of Venus de Milo

During a time when many were giving their homes over

to house soldiers or nurse the wounded, the nation's largest museum did the same, as the article noted: "The upper stories of the Louvre…have been converted into hospital wards for the Red Cross and now there is not a vestige of the beautiful works of art that once were grouped about the halls. Some of the soldiers who were first sent to the front were recalled and set as guards in the Louvre."

Fortunately, the end of the war brought about a new era of prosperity and interest in art and culture. Though the museum did not necessarily acquire any major pieces between World War I and World War II, its reputation as a major landmark made it a necessary stop for anyone touring Europe. Writing in the American *Western Weekly Magazine* in 1930, James Abbe opined, "The Louvre gets further under [one's] skin than 'ruins,' 'battle fields' or ancient hostelries which are quaint but lack bathrooms. When all is said and done, the Louvre is rather a gay place. The morgue-like atmosphere of some art museums is not to be found there. Movement, life, the mingling of nationalities, races and tongues, synchronize well with the air of successful effort which radiates from the works of dead and gone artists and craftsmen…The Louvre just impresses the visiting American as an endless series of shop windows in which are displayed stimulating and often gay paintings, most lifelike and unashamed statues of quite nude men and women, jewelry, furniture, tapestries, ship models, clocks, snuff boxes, none of which could be purchased at any price."

Of course, peace proved short-lived again, and as much of Europe began to prepare for another war with Germany, so did the Louvre. As soon as word reached the museum about the occupation of the Sudetenland, the directors shipped the "Mona Lisa" and a number of other major works to the Château de Chambord in the Loire Valley for safekeeping. When Germany invaded Poland a year later, most of the rest of the collections were also sent there, where they remained until after the war.

Manfred Heyde's picture of the Château de Chambord

Following World War II, the Louvre faced a new challenge. During the Nazi occupation, the Germans had stolen more than 150,000 of pieces of art, many of them from Jewish families sent to concentration camps, so when the war ended, the Allies found much of the art in storage, while thousands of others were apparently burned or kept by individual soldiers and smuggled home to family members. Those items which remained needed to be returned to their rightful owners, but this was easier said than done, especially since entire extended families had been wiped out and those who did survive could not necessarily prove ownership of any given piece.

In the meantime, the items awaiting return needed to be properly stored and cared for, so the Allies turned more than 61,000 of them over to the Louvre for safekeeping, and the museum put them on display in 1946 in the hopes that they would be reclaimed by either the individuals or the institutions that rightfully owned them. One story of lost treasures that were rediscovered appeared in the *Syracuse Post Standard* on October 22, 1950: "Eleven oil paintings, part of a collection of 78 which were recovered from the Nazis thru the alertness of the custodian of the Louvre Museum, have been put on display at Colgate University for their first American showing. The paintings are the property of Dr. Stefan Osusky, former Czechoslovakian ambassador to France…. At the time of the German invasion to Paris, Dr. Osusky…fled to London…. Before leaving, he hit upon a plan to safeguard his collection from the plundering Nazis. To prevent informers from leading the invaders to the hiding place of the paintings, he engaged one trucking firm to cart them to a vacant warehouse, then had them transferred to another firm and whisked away to the eventual hiding place."

Unfortunately, Dr. Osusky's plan proved only a partial success. The article continued, "It was not until 1943 that Goering's "art collectors" traced down the first firm, and not until 1944 that the paintings were finally unearthed.

Anticipating their withdrawal that same year in the face of the Allied invasion, the Germans loaded 52 freight cars with rare art works, including Dr. Osusky's 100 pieces. French railroad men, however, learned the content of the cars and shunted them about so they never reached Germany."

Finally, the war ended and the search began for rightful owners. The article concluded, "The task of recovering the stolen art was started after the war by the Louvre Museum, and it was there that the custodian…came upon a portrait of Madame Osusky, who was known to him thru visits to the Czech embassy. Mme. Osusky…finally identified 78 of the paintings. No trace of the other 22 has been found. Dr. Osusky apparently has written them off as having been taken singly by German occupation officials and transported in widely-scattered areas in Germany."

In 1949, four years after the war had ended, about 2,100 pieces remained unclaimed, approximately half of them paintings. Of these, a quarter or more had likely come from Jewish families. Between 1950 and 1954, they were exhibited again, but only a handful of pieces were claimed. Most of the unclaimed pieces remain in the museum to this day, as time has made it increasingly difficult to locate those to whom they likely belonged. In 1997, the French government appointed a Commission, led by Jean Mattéoli, to assess the art pieces left, and the commission reported back that the museum still has 678 unclaimed pieces of artwork in its collection. There have been no new claims of ownership since 2006.

The post-World War II Era has witnessed remarkable changes in both the meaning of art and the purpose of museums. Although France continued to move on and rebuild, reminders of the war's tolls were everywhere, and recovering from the losses suffered took much of the nation's time and budget. It was not until the early 1980s that the museum was ready for another major building project; in 1984, French President Francois Mitterrand commissioned architect I.M. Pei to design a metal and glass pyramid as a centerpiece to the museum's main entrance. The structure rises 71 feet into the air and has a spacious lobby that funnels visitors into the museum at a slower pace and thereby allows for improved crowd control.

Pei

The Louvre Pyramid

The pyramid was dogged by controversy from the beginning, and when it opened to the public on March 30, 1989, the *New York Times* reported, "When Mitterrand selected Pei in 1983 to design the Grand Louvre — to give air, space and light to one of the world's most congested museums — his popularity was at rock bottom, and political sniping was intense. The triumph in 1986 of a conservative coalition in parliamentary elections posed new perils to the Grand Louvre, and then-Finance Minister Edouard Bahadur refused to move out of his offices to make way for Pei's workmen. The right-wing press, led by the daily Le Figaro, lambasted the idea of shattering the harmony of the Louvre's courtyard with a glass iceberg."

The controversy put pressure on everyone involved to finish the job quickly and efficiently. Leonard Jacobson, one of the architects who worked on the structure, recalled, "We had tremendous pressure to get the pyramid itself accelerated, to get it to be what the French call irreversible. You don't build the top first, but that's what we had to do."

Ultimately, the opening itself was a success, with the *Times* reporting, "But Wednesday afternoon, with the sun showing off the pyramid at its glittering best, the dispute over the pyramid's esthetic merits seemed over. The crowds and even formerly critical cognoscenti gave it rave reviews. Many non-cognoscenti who spilled down the curving stairway into the underground complex were startled by its size, by its airy lightness and by the unique, almost underwater views it afforded of the Louvre looming above, captured through the main pyramid and three mini-pyramids added to draw in light."

The pyramid is, in many ways, a symbol of the Louvre itself, and its ongoing efforts to keep up with both tradition and changing times. A 2001 article in *Newsweek* magazine noted, "Pierre Rosenberg began working at the Musée du Louvre in 1961, and for the last seven years served as director until his government-imposed retirement in April on the eve of his 65th birthday. During those 40 years, Rosenberg witnessed great changes in everything from why people go to museums to how the museums themselves look and are run." Rosenberg himself insisted, "We need to bring people back to museums, and not only to see the '"Mona Lisa".' How many people have returned to museums because they discovered their beauty and pleasure? Very few, I suspect. …works of art are not easy to understand. And I think this is a real issue for the future. Until now there was art education in schools. You had a little bit of knowledge about antiquity and Old and New Testament. Now this knowledge is lost all over the world."

Expressing his concerns that interest in the Louvre's world famous permanent collection had given way to public fascination with travelling exhibits, he continued, "At the beginning, we thought at the Louvre…that there was enough in a museum, and that the exhibitions should be in another place. Now we know that to get people back to museums you need to have events." He explained that there were three reasons why the museum needed to acquire new pieces: "First, because tastes change and one has to take into account what becomes fashionable. … Second, a museum has to tell a story. The Louvre…can really tell the story of painting from the beginning until the period that the museum stops its purpose. … And third, the richness of a country depends on its capacity to keep what has been brought to the country in the past."

Toward the end of 2002, Museum Director Henri Lourette recalled, "I remember when I was younger, the Louvre collection was open to the public, but there was no restaurant and no visitor center. Everything around the museum has developed in the last 25 years, as our idea of what a museum provides has changed. The profile of a director has changed as well because the idea of the museum changed."

One of the major issues facing the Louvre in the early 21st century was the matter of who would be in charge of it: the French government or the museum board. Lourette continued, "It became a "Public Administration Establishment" in 1993. For us, autonomy means the administration can manage the organization, the employees, and scientific development. Reports have been written which bring up certain points. It's a nonpolitical discussion on structural questions, supported not just by the Louvre, but also by the National Assembly, the Cour des Comptes [the state auditing agency], all of which emphasized the importance of the Louvre's autonomy…Until next year, we don't have direct control of employment and recruitment of about two-thirds of our staff. That's one of the reasons why 26% of our galleries are closed every day. As of Jan. 1, 2003, we will have direct control of some of the personnel, including the security staff. That will allow us to resolve some problems more quickly, like the closed galleries. It will reinforce the legitimacy of the museum's direction. We're also working toward more financial autonomy."

One of the most important issues facing the museum, and Europe in general, is the large wave of immigrants who have come in the last decade. They are shaping both the political and the cultural landscape of the museum, and in 2012, the Louvre opened a new gallery dedicated exclusively to Islamic art. The *Associated Press* reported on September 30, "In its boldest development in a generation, the Louvre Museum has a new wing dedicated to Islamic art, a nearly $130 million project that comes at a tense time between the West and the Muslim world. Louvre curators tout their new Islamic art department, which took 11 years to build and was opened to the public Sept. 22, as a way to help bridge cultural divides…The galleries provide a needed showcase one of the West's most extensive Islamic art collections, some 18,000 artifacts that range from the seventh century to the 19th century. But the wing does not dwell on the old: It is housed under a futuristic, undulating glass roof designed by architects Rudy Ricciotti and Mario Bellini that has garnered comparisons to a dragonfly wing, a flying carpet, even a wind-blown veil…The Louvre collection's mission is to foster understanding between the West and the Islamic world. Instead of highlighting Islam as one united religion, it celebrates the secular, tolerant and cultural aspects of different Islamic civilizations. … The Louvre opened a department of Islamic art in 2003, under former President Jacques Chirac, who said he wanted to highlight the contributions of Muslim civilizations to Western culture."

Speaking about the new hall, Islamic Art Department head Sophie Makariou explained, "I like the idea of showing the other side of the coin. We are talking about a diverse world that goes from the Atlantic, Spain and Morocco to India. It brings complexity. We are suffering from simplistic views on the Islamic world. (Some) would make us believe that there is just one Islam, which is just not true."

The Louvre's Art Departments

Jorge Royan's picture of a restoration workshop in the Louvre

Today, the Musée du Louvre consists of eight departments caring for 380,000 pieces of art, less than 10% of which are on display at any given time.

Among its oldest pieces are those brought back by Napoleon and others from Egypt; among the 50,000 pieces in the collection are items from the Nile region that date back as far as 4000 BCE. Charles X ordered the Egyptian Department created after Jean-Francois Champollion translated the Rosette Stone in the early 19th century and convinced Charles to buy 7,000 more items from three different collections. Among the items housed in the Paris museum are carefully preserved items of clothing and jewelry, games played by children and adults alike, mummies, musical instruments, papyrus scrolls, tools and weapons.

The Egyptian Department is also one of the most controversial in the Louvre, primarily because of the way much of the collection came into its possession. In addition to conquest, many of its treasures were purchased from sources that had obtained them through less-than-honorable or legal means. In 2009, according to an October 11 *Associated Press* article, "France's culture minister agreed Friday to return five painted wall fragments to Egypt after a row over their ownership prompted the Egyptians to cut ties with the Louvre Museum. A committee of 35 specialists unanimously recommended that France give back the painted wall fragments from a 3,200-year-old tomb near the ancient temple city of Luxor. … [Culture Minister Frederic] Mitterrand said the items were acquired by the Louvre in 'good faith' and that the decision to return them reflects France's and the Louvre's commitment of 'resolute action against illegal trafficking of cultural goods.'"

The article continued with information given by Zahi Hawass, Egypt's Antiquites Chief: "In a statement Friday, Hawass' office said that ties would not be restored until the five fragments were returned to Egypt and that France would not be allowed to conduct archaeological activity until then. Thousands of antiquities were spirited out of the country during Egypt's colonial period and afterward by archaeologists, adventurers and thieves. … Those at issue now, however, were obtained relatively recently. Hawass' office said thieves chipped them from the walls of the tomb near the Valley of the Kings in the 1980s. The Louvre bought them in 2000 and 2003."

One of the other most important departments is the one housing items from the Near East, including Ancient Mesopotamia and Iran, many of which came to Paris in the mid-1840s thanks to the work of Paul-Emile Botta. The Code of Hammurabi plays an important role in this exhibit as an example of one of the earliest versions of codified law. Although Hammurabi's law code is the most famous of the Mesopotamian law codes, it was not the first; the tradition of law codes being written and published by Mesopotamian kings had been well established in the Sumerian tradition, and Hammurabi simply carried that tradition over to the Akkadian language. The first attested Sumerian law code now extant is that of Ur-Namma, king of Ur, and dates from around 2100 BCE. Slightly closer in time and geography to Hammurabi was the law code of Lipit-Ištar of Isin circa 1930 BCE. But of course, the fact Hammurabi's was found at a critical time in the development of historical studies has helped ensure the popularity of the code and the man himself.

The Code of Hammurabi

The third department is devoted to the Greeks, Romans and Etruscans. Beginning with the Cycladic period, the items stretch to the time of the Roman Empire. While the Egyptian department contains the oldest pieces, the Greek, Etruscan and Roman area houses the first items acquired by the French for display, including a number of objects that came to France during the reign of Francis I. Most of the items in this collection consist of large, marble statuary and small, delicate jewelry. There is also a good deal of pottery and some items worked in brass.

The fourth collection in the museum has already been mentioned. The Islamic act collection claims proudly that is spans "thirteen hundred years of history and three continents, reflecting the creativity and diversity of inspiration in Islamic countries." It includes more than 6,000 complete and partial pieces of ceramics and glass, as well as ivory, metalware, and wood. Perhaps even more interesting, there are a number of ancient textiles, including carpets, and a wide variety of miniatures.

While the first four departments are classified primarily by the era or inspiration behind their collections, the other four departments are divided according to the medium used by each artist in his or her piece. First there is the sculpture collection, made up of three-dimensional art pieces created before 1850 but not by ancient peoples. It began in 1824 when the museum displayed for the first time two pieces by Michelangelo: Dying Slave and Rebellious Slave. Because of the size of many of the objects in the collection, they were initially few in number, but in 1847, Leon Laborde took over the department and began building up the collection, focusing much of his attention on medieval art. The collection now takes up two sections of the museum, with French pieces in one wing and all others in a second wing.

Jorg Bittner Unna's picture of Dying Slave

Jorg Bittner Unna's picture of Rebellious Slave

The Louvre's sixth department, that of objets d'art, contains items from around the Middle Ages to 1850. Originally part of the sculpture department, it was made independent in the early 19th century and contains small items of glass and bronze, as well as a wide selection of jewelry. The department also houses one of the world's most complete collections of faience, a type of Italian pottery glazed with tin. These items are on display in the Richelieu Wing and the Apollo Gallery. The department also contains a number of tapestries that are displayed in the Chagoury Gallery.

A picture of the exterior of the Richelieu Wing

For all that they make up only one department in the vast museum, it goes without saying that the paintings in the Louvre are what the museum is best known for. 12 full time curators care for its 7,500+ canvases, which date from the 13th century to 1848. About 5,000 of the pieces were painted by French artists, 1,200 are from Northern Europe, and the rest come from elsewhere around the world. In 1986, museum officials decided the 1848 Revolution would be the cutoff point for items remaining in the Louvre; works created after that date were moved to the Musée d'Orsay, on the Left Bank. In 1869, Louis La Caze left the largest single collection of paintings to the Louvre, consisting of 584 pieces from his personal collection.

The final department is that of prints and drawings, consisting of more than 75,000 items, most of them originally from the Royal Collection. This department consists of three sections: the 415 items in the *Cabinet de Roi*, another 14,000 copper printing plates used to mass produce items, and thousands of prints, drawings and books donated by Edmond de Rothchild. The items are displayed for only brief periods of time due to their fragility, and they can be seen in the *Pavillon de Flore*.

The Louvre's Most Famous Works

Ask almost anyone about the Louvre and the "Mona Lisa" will inevitably come up in the conversation. Jean-

Pierre Cuzin, himself a curator at the Louvre, explains the reason: "The entire history of portraiture afterwards depends on the "Mona Lisa". If you look at all the other portraits – not only of the Italian Renaissance, but also of the seventeenth to nineteenth centuries – if you look at Picasso, at everyone you want to name, all of them were inspired by this painting. Thus it is sort of the root, almost, of occidental portrait painting…Today's art critics call attention to the painting's mystery and harmony. But the first art historians to describe it emphasized its striking realism, pointing out 'the lips that smile' and 'the eyes that shine.'" Cuzin is hardly the only one with such a view; Leonardo's biographer Giorgio Vasari noted, "As art may imitate nature, she does not appear to be painted, but truly of flesh and blood. On looking closely at the pit of her throat, one could swear that the pulses were beating."

Vasari definitely hit on something here, for, as Cuzin points out, "Leonardo has studied the sky, the elements, the atmosphere, and the light. He takes the approach of a scientist, but translates it into the painting with superb delicacy and finesse. For him the painting doesn't count. What counts is the knowledge. In the same painting we move from soft places like the clouds to areas of extreme intricacy and fine detail." As an example, he points out that "around the neckline of the lady's dress we have delicate interlacing embroidery. The contrast of these different areas creates a cohesion that is very rare in painting. … The background may be a representation of the universe, with mountains, plains and rivers. Or possibly it is both reality and the world of dream. One could suppose that the landscape doesn't exist, that it is the young woman's own dream world."

If the "Mona Lisa" is famed for its beauty and serenity, "The Raft of the Medusa" is just the opposite, for it depicts one of the most tragic events in French maritime history. According to reporter Anthony Peregrine, "Two hundred years ago, 147 French sailors and maritime passengers were cast adrift on a raft off west Africa. They ended up fighting, killing, and eating the dead. … Scandal and uproar ensued in post-Napoleonic France. …the episode inspired one of the greatest, and biggest, paintings of the 19th century…27-year-old Théodore Géricault saw his chance to make a name by committing the tragedy to enormous canvas. His preparations were prodigious. He interviewed survivors, visited morgues to get the right deathly skin pallor and filled his flat with body parts (including a severed head from a lunatic asylum) to act as 'models'. Finished in 1819, the painting found some favor in France, much more in a London invariably thrilled by evidence of killer French bungling. Ultimately, "The Raft of the Medusa" entered the Louvre only after Géricault's early death…in 1824. There it remains, immensely more overwhelming than any image…. Experts will tell you it's an evolution of classicism towards romanticism. I'll tell you that there's so much going on, the work threatens to surge from the frame and sweep you away."

"The Raft of the Medusa"

"The Seated Scribe" is not only one of the most popular works in the Louvre but also one of the oldest, dating from the Fourth Dynasty in Egypt (between 2600 and 2500 BCE). Writing for the Louvre's own website, authors Sophie Labbé-Toutée and Christiane Ziegler observed, "The Louvre's scribe, known as the 'Seated Scribe', is indeed sitting cross-legged, his right leg crossed in front of his left. The white kilt, stretched over his knees, serves as a support. He is holding a partially rolled papyrus scroll in his left hand. His right hand must have held a brush, now missing…The most striking aspect of this sculpture is the face, particularly the elaborately inlaid eyes: they consist of a piece of red-veined white magnesite, in which a piece of slightly truncated rock crystal was placed. The front part of the crystal was carefully polished. The back side was covered with a layer of organic material, creating the color of the iris and also probably serving as an adhesive. The entire eye was then held in the socket by two large copper clips welded on the back. A line of black paint defines the eyebrows. The hands, fingers, and fingernails are sculpted with a remarkable delicacy. His chest is broad and the nipples are marked by two wooden dowels…the statue of the scribe was apparently discovered in Saqqara on 19 November 1850, to the north of the Serapeum's line of sphinxes. But the precise location is not known…. Some historians have tried to link it to one of the owners of the statues discovered at the same time." This leaves the question of who exactly the scribe is supposed to represent. They continue: "The most convincing of these associates the scribe to Pehernefer. … The statue of Pehernefer dates from the 4th Dynasty. This is an additional argument in favor of an earlier dating for this statue, which has sometimes been dated to the 6th Dynasty. Another argument supporting this date is that 'writing' scribes were mostly created in the 4th and early

5th Dynasties; after this period, most scribes were portrayed in 'reading' poses."

G. Baotic's picture of The Seated Scribe

While "Death of Sardanapalus," created by Eugène Delacroix in 1827, is popular today and considered one of the most important works in the Louvre, it was looked upon with some disdain when the museum purchased it in 1921. In a special dispatch, one reporter complained, "Is the reputation of the Louvre as the future art centre of the world to be based on the fact that the paintings exhibited are the most expensive obtainable instead of being of real artistic merit?" The same reporter then warned, "French critics profess to see in the acquisition of Delacroix's 'Death of Sardanapalus' evidence of this tendency, for although last month the Louvre paid 700,000 francs for the painting, which is twelve by fifteen feet, it was so lightly considered by art experts thirty years ago that it could have been bought for less than 80,000 francs…The Delacroix work was first exhiblted in the salon in 1827, when it was ridiculed by visitors and critics. For fifty-five years it remained in the Wilson collection, when it was sold for 95,000 francs to an amateur, who, when tried to sell it, could not get more than 60,000 francs. M. Haro, its next owner, sold it in 1892 for less than 30,000 francs, after failing to receive a single offer at a public auction attended by museum buyers from England, Italy, France and the United States."

"Death of Sardanapalus"

  Naturally, items in the art world flow in and out of favor as times and tastes change, and this trend can perhaps most clearly be seen in "Sleeping Hermaphroditus," a Roman copy of a 2nd century CE bronze executed in stone by Gianlorenzo Bernini in 1619. Writing on this item for the *New York Times* in 2016, Daniel McDermon told readers, "Gender and sexual identity are on many minds right now. There are continuing legal battles over bathroom access; piles of gossip items about Caitlyn Jenner…. For those used to dividing the world neatly into male and female, the new way of thinking feels, well, new. But, of course, these complexities are as old as humanity…In 2016, embracing the ambiguities of gender and sexual identity can be a way to signal open-mindedness. And even in this, ancient civilizations were ahead of us. … In imperial Rome, sculptures like this filled the homes and gardens of wealthy people…. They were seen as light amusements, signifiers of good taste. And it is believed that there were hundreds of them because at least nine copies of the "Sleeping Hermaphrodite" have survived." He then observed, "The best-known sleeping hermaphrodite, now at the Louvre, was unearthed in Rome in 1608. The billowy mattress was an addition, added by the sculptor Gian Lorenzo Bernini at the request of the work's then owner, Cardinal Scipione Borghese."

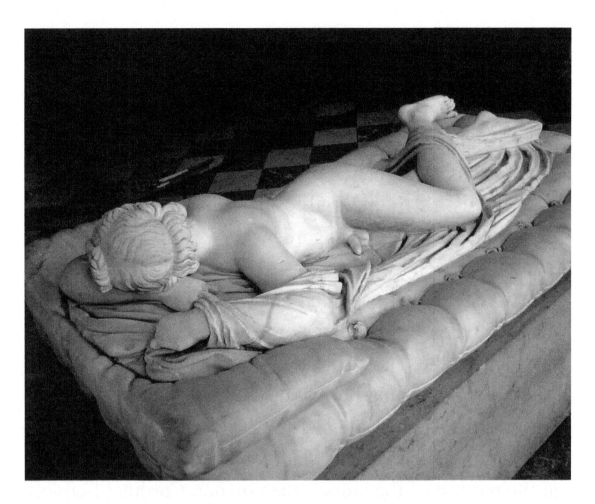

Sleeping Hermaphroditus

In 2017, the "Venus de Milo" has had the dubious honor of being featured in a television advertisement for Greek yogurt, but while this hardly seems to be an appropriate use for such an ancient work of art, it is likely not the worst thing that has happened to the piece since it was created in the 1ˢᵗ century BCE. Writing in 2015, historian Elizabeth Nix observed, "One of the most famous examples of ancient Greek sculpture, the Venus de Milo is immediately recognizable by its missing arms and popularly believed to represent Aphrodite, the Greek goddess of love and beauty, who was known to the Romans as Venus."

She went on to tell the story of how the statue came to her famous home: "The artwork was discovered in 1820 on the Aegean island of Melos (also called Milos). An ensign in the French navy, Olivier Voutier…decided to [go] ashore…searching for antiquities. While digging near the ruins of an ancient theater, Voutier noticed that a local farmer…seemed to have found something inside the wall. Upon investigating, Voutier learned the farmer had located the top half of a statue of a woman. Recognizing the statue as potentially significant, the Frenchman…unearthed its lower half not far away…Voutier told his superiors about the discovery and the French acquired the artwork…for a relatively modest sum. It arrived in France in 1821 and was presented to Louis XVIII, who donated it to the Louvre Museum. … Originally carved in two blocks of marble then fitted together, the statue stands 6 feet 7 inches from head to toe and is the creation of an artist named Alexandros of Antioch, about whom little is known."

Two of the more moving statues are those of the "Dying Slave" and the "Rebellious Slave" created by Michelangelo between 1513 and 1516. According to reporter Lauren Mitchell Ruehring, "Dying Slave was created between 1513 and 1516. Together with Rebellious

Slave, it was meant for the tomb of Julius II but was not included because of lack of space. Eventually given away by the master, Dying Slave and Rebellious Slave reveal the artist's approach to sculpting. Michelangelo visualized the figures as imprisoned in the huge blocks of marble, and only by carefully removing the excess stone could he free them. In their creation, and in their final impact, the two slaves may symbolize the soul's struggle against the bonds of temptation and sin…Dying Slave seems to be sinking into a deep sleep. Far from dying, the figure in Michelangelo's Dying Slave seems to be abandoning himself to the effects of an intoxicant. Little resistance is shown in the silky contours of the arched back, extended left arm, and relaxed abdomen."

  On the other hand, Ruehring noted, "Rebellious Slave…is engaged in a far more active struggle than its counterpart. The contrast between Rebellious Slave and Dying Slave skillfully shows human resistance to the chains of bondage and the temptation to submit to the inevitable. Compare also the roughly hewn surfaces of Rebellious Slave to the highly polished finish of Dying Slave." Finally, "The extraordinarily powerful torso, straining its hulking mass of bone and flesh against bands that tie it back, seems more animal than human. Using sweeping, brushlike strokes made by a three-toothed chisel, Michelangelo created a Rebellious Slave that is lacking the definition of his earlier sculptures and seems instead to express in its coarse surface the very essence of agonized humanity."

It should not be surprising to modern readers that the common thread in many of the most popular pieces in the Louvre is a certain sexual mystery. This powerful tension between "loves me/loves me not" has been at the heart of controversy since the beginning of time. However, rarely is it more clearly displayed, or perhaps more accurately, unclearly displayed, than in "La Grande Odalisque" by Jean Auguste Dominique Ingres. Created in 1814, the painting clearly leaves the viewer wondering, as one whimsical person put it, "is her glance saying come-hither or get lost?" Another author commented, "It has been noted by some art historians that the elongation of the odalisque's back and pelvic area were not only drawn to satisfy Ingres' quest for an ideal form of the female body. Ingres was well-known for the way in which he reflected his subject's social condition through his paintings…As it was the odalisque's duty to satisfy the carnal pleasures of the sultan, this elongation of her pelvic area may have been a symbolic distortion by Ingres. She lies on the divan, her nudity a signal that she is offering herself. She is described as a modest harem, as only her back and part of one breast is shown. But if one looks closely to her face, it seems aloof and absent of any sign of eager expectations…By the time Ingres produced La Grande Odalisque aged 34 he should have been used to the harsh reaction of critics. The work Ingres exhibited at earlier salons was ridiculed but his exhibition of La Grande Odalisque at the Salon of 1819 proved the most shocking. Critics were outraged by the display of Ingres' wild imagination. This piece was received more positively after his death, influencing great artists as Degas and Picasso. Today, it invokes a positive response and is looked upon as one of Ingres' most memorable works."

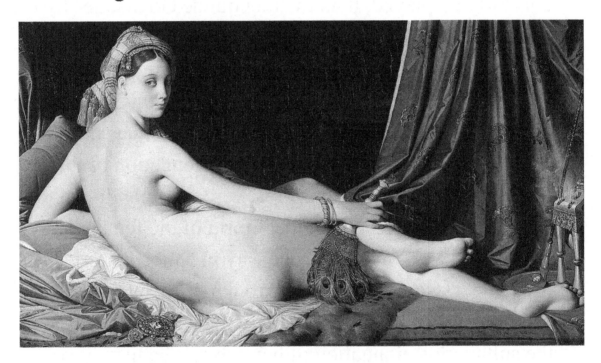

"La Grande Odalisque"

It is important to remember that not all the paintings in the Louvre are on canvas. 'Venus and the Three Graces Presenting Gifts to a Young Woman" is a well-known fresco created by Sandro Botticelli between 1483 and

1486. He originally painted it on plaster freshly applied to the walls of the Tuscan Villa Lemmi, located outside Florence, Italy, along with "A Young Man Being Introduced to the Seven Liberal Arts." The fresco, commissioned by Giovanni Tornabuoni in honor of his son's marriage, shows Venus and the Graces presenting gifts to the young bride, including roses, the Western symbol of love and beauty. When the paintings were discovered in 1873, they had been whitewashed over. The museum transferred the frescoes to canvas for support and moved them to the Louvre, where they were cleaned and put on display.

'Venus and the Three Graces Presenting Gifts to a

"A Young Man Being Introduced to the Seven Liberal Arts"

One of the earliest masterpieces to find widespread public favor was "Bathsheba at Her Bath" from 1654. As one author noted, "Rembrandt was undoubtedly the first painter to have made the soul and its expression the purpose of his art. He comes at the end of the age of humanism, in the sense that his subjects are most often taken from the Old or New Testament. His work is steeped in the collective consciousness, whose traditional religious themes he interprets with an unprecedented depth of understanding. In him Christian inspiration is given perhaps its most sublime expression equal, at the very least, to that of the Middle Ages…And whether he paints portraits, nudes, or Biblical scenes — his Bathsheba combines all three — he always glorifies humanity and the love and goodness which bind men together. Nevertheless, while giving eloquent expression to the age of humanism, he also introduces the age of individualism. From the very start he imbues it with a note of astonishing intensity, for it was by exploring himself that he acquired the power of affecting other men."

"Bathsheba at Her Bath"

One cannot depart from the Egyptian section of the Louvre without stopping by to see the Great Sphinx of Tanis, constructed around 2600 BCE in Egypt. Some say it is the guardian of the museum, and it is certainly a formidable piece, one whose very presence symbolizes the early years of the museum's development. It was excavated by Napoleon's men in 1825 and is one of the largest sphinxes still in existence outside of Egypt. Not surprisingly, it is one of the most popular stops along any tour of the great museum.

The Great Sphinx of Tanis

Among the most popular pieces at the Louvre is "The Wedding at Cana" by Veronese. Writing for the *New York Times* in 1992, Marlise Simons explained, "Veronese's monumental work, measuring 22 by 32 1/2 feet, is one of the largest paintings in the Louvre and is considered one of the museum's greatest Renaissance treasures. The grand biblical feast with its rich textures and more than 120 figures is regarded as one of the masterpieces of the Venetian school." The article continued, "Napoleon ordered the Veronese brought to France as war booty. When his envoys plucked the work from the wall in the abbey of San Giorgio Maggiore in Venice, they cut it in half for the journey to Paris. Once patched up, it spent months packed in a box in the port of Brest during the Franco-Prussian War of 1870-71. The canvas was once more rolled up and hidden in World War II, when it was hauled around France on a truck to keep it from the Germans."

"The Wedding at Cana"

There are few items in the Louvre as impressive as the

Code of Hammurabi from the late 1700s BCE in Mesopotamia. This is one of the earliest records of codified law, and one that has survived the longest in fact. Its text covered everything from economic laws to the idea that a man is presumed innocent until proven guilty. It also lays out how a case should be tried in court, including the idea that both the accuser and the accused should have the right to make their case before the people, and it insists that punishments should be adjusted according to the background and opportunities of the one convicted. The stele, shaped like a large, seven foot tall index finger, is carved in cuneiform script with most of the entire text of the laws, written in Akkadian. It was discovered by archaeologists in 1901 and translated the following year by Jean-Vincent Scheil.

Another important piece is the Lamassu from 7th Century BCE Mesopotamia. Author William Robinson later described his first encounter with this unique work: "And here I finally was, in the Louvre, in front of the inscribed lamassu, the great winged bulls with human heads dug up by Botta. The Assyrians were superstitious folk and placed these huge sculptures at doorways to ward off evil spirits." In fact, these lions not only had wings but also five legs, giving the impression that they are actually walking, not standing still. Yet they did stand still, at attention, for decades, in front of the Mesopotamian capital of Sargon II.

The Met's Early Years

By the early 19th century, the Louvre in Paris had developed a reputation across Europe for both the quality and quantity of its holdings, making it the world's most famous art museum. Writing in 1814, Sir Archibald Alison claimed, "For an attempt of this kind, the Louvre presents singular advantages, from the unparalleled collection of paintings of every school and description which are there to be met with, and the facility with which you can there trace the progress of the art from its first beginning to the period of its greatest perfection…And it is in this view that the collection of these works into one museum, however much to be deplored as the work of unprincipled ambition, and however much it may have diminished the impression which particular objects, from the influence of association, produced in their native place, is yet calculated to produce the greatest of all improvements in the progress of the art…by divesting particular schools and particular works of the unbounded influence which the effect of early association, or the prejudices of national feeling, have given them in their original situation, and placing them where their real nature is to be judged of by a more extended circle, and subjected to the examination of more impartial sentiments."

Thus, it should come as little surprise that the concept for a large, prestigious art museum was devised in Paris, the cultural and artistic heart of Europe. On July 4, 1869, a group of Americans met together in the French capital to celebrate the anniversary of America's independence, and during the meeting, the issue of American culture arose. Years later, John Jay, a man described by one author as "ceaseless in good works," recalled, "The simple suggestion that 'it was time for the American people to lay the foundation of a National Institution and Gallery of Art and that the American gentlemen then in Europe were the men to inaugurate the plan' commended itself to a number of the gentlemen present, who formed themselves into a committee for inaugurating the movement."

Their work paid off, and on April 13, 1870, the New York State Legislature voted into law an Act of Incorporation for an institution called the Metropolitan Museum of Art in New York City. The stated purpose of this organization, according to the Act, was for "establishing and maintaining in said City a Museum and Library of Art, of encouraging and developing the Study of the Fine Arts, and the application of Art to manufacture and natural life, of advancing the general knowledge of kindred subjects, and to that end of furnishing popular instruction and recreations." The first president, American businessman John Taylor Johnston, and the other officers were already in place, having been elected the previous January. On May 24, they held their first annual meeting and adopted a permanent constitution. They also committed themselves to raising $250,000 with which to build a museum and purchase collections.

Johnston

In the meanwhile, the museum's first piece, a Roman sarcophagus found in Tarsus, arrived as a gift from J. Abdo Debbas, a native of Adana in southern Turkey and the American vice-consul in Tarsus. Debbas had discovered the sarcophagus in 1863 and was anxious to make a gift of it to the United States government. Since the government itself could not accept such an offering, J. Augustus Johnson, the American consul in Beirut, advised him to donate to the newly formed museum. It took 16 buffaloes to pull the wagon carrying the sarcophagus to the port at Mersin, where it was shipped to America.

By the time the sarcophagus arrived in New York, William Blodgett had worked with John Taylor Johnston to purchase 174 paintings for the museum's new collection, many of which remain housed at the Met today. This was something of a leap of faith, as the museum had not yet raised even half of the money it needed to open. However, plans went forth and the state legislature passed another act, with this one mandating that the new museum would be built "upon that portion of Central Park formerly known as Manhattan Square, or any other park, square or place."

Blodgett

One of Blodgett's most famous contributions,
***Alexander and Diogenes* by Caspar de Crayer**

Having a site for the building proved to be the turning point. After that, money began to pour in, and by 1872, the Board of Directors already had more pledges than it had previously hoped to get. With these promises in hand, it leased the Dodworth Building on Fifth Avenue as a temporary site for the museum, and there, on February 20, 1872, the museum opened its first exhibit. John Taylor Johnston described the opening to a friend: "We had a fine turnout of ladies and gentlemen and all were highly pleased. The pictures looked splendidly and compliments were so plenty and strong that I was afraid the mouths of the Trustees would become chronically and permanently fixed in a broad grin. The Loan Committee worked hard at the last and got together a few things of interest, and perhaps it was as well that at the first there should be little to take off the attention from the pictures and also that we should be able to announce from time to time additions to the Loan Exhibition."

NEW YORK CITY.—OPENING RECEPTION OF THE METROPOLITAN MUSEUM OF ART, AT THE TEMPORARY HALL, NO. 681 FIFTH AVENUE, FEBRUARY 20TH.

An engraving of the opening

As for the exhibits themselves, Johnston conceded that they were a mixed bag at best. He explained, "Vela's

Napoleon was in place and looked splendidly and excited universal admiration. It is better, if anything, than the original and the marble is perfect. I saw it myself, for the first time, on the reception evening and was perfectly satisfied. We have secured but not yet put up Mr. Alden's fine woodwork. It is much finer than we had supposed, having only before seen it in the cellar. The Westchester Apollo turns out to be three feet high, a statuette. We decided, however, to take it. Mr. Rowe presents us with a colossal dancing girl by Schwanthaler, the celebrated German sculptor at Munich. It may be very fine, but eight feet of dance is a trial to the feelings…we must curb the exuberance of donors except in the article of money, of which latter they may give as much as they please…The sarcophagus has not yet been moved up but will be soon. I think I wrote you that Sturgis on examination liked it very much. J. Augustus Johnson (the donor) has since seen it and pronounces it a fine specimen of the later Roman and probably a royal tomb. It will be more carefully examined when 'in situ.'" Ultimately, "We may now consider the Museum fairly launched and under favorable auspices. People were generally surprised, and agreeably so, to find what we had. No one had imagined that we could make such a show, and the disposition to praise is now as general as the former disposition to depreciate. We have now something to point to as the Museum, something tangible and something good. The cry of humbug can hardly be raised now by anyone."

Later that year, the museum began a series of lectures, with Hiram Hitchcock delivering the first on recent discoveries made by General Luigi di Cesnola in Cyprus. More importantly, the Trustees settled on placing the Met along five blocks in Central Park, between 79th and 84th Streets.

In 1873, the Met moved to another temporary location, this time the Douglas Mansion on West 14th Street, where those in charge opened an exhibit presenting Cesnola's collection, thereby exhausting the remainder of the $250,000 raised. The state legislature then chipped in by voting to allow the museum to apply for up to $15,000 each year to maintain the building and exhibits, and the following year the museum was able to purchase Cesnola's collection. Cesnola would later go on to serve on the board of the museum, beginning in 1877.

Luigi di Cesnola, the first Director of the Met

By this time, the museum was established enough to begin to attract the work of some popular modern artists, and when he died in 1872, John Kensett left the Met a large number of his original works. According to one journalist, "His style evolved from the first generation of the Hudson River School style into what is known as Luminism. The Luminists in general focused on light and atmosphere, instead of painting specific topographical locations, and Kensett more than any of the other artists pursued this "negative space" tendency towards abstraction. When he died in 1872, after rescuing neighbor Vincent Colyer's wife from drowning in long Island Sound, his studio was discovered to contain a series of not quite finished paintings, since titled "Last Summer's

Work." They stunned the New York art world and were regarded as absolute works of genius. They were so well thought of that the infant Metropolitan Museum of Art, an institution Kensett and his fellow Union League Club members founded, made a group of 39 landscapes of Lake George, and Long Island Sound the nucleus of its painting collection."

Kensett

***The Old Pine, Darien, Connecticut*, one of Kensett's paintings housed at the Met**

While the $15,000 would help balance the books, the Trustees knew they would need more money as time went on, so they decided to start charging admission for the exhibits. That said, to make sure that everyone, no matter what their income, could enjoy the contents of the museum, they decided to refrain from charging admissions on Mondays. Two years later, they would make Thursday free, also. The museum also issued its first guide to the exhibits, an important step toward fulfilling the educational task it had been given by the legislature.

New Digs

In 1876, people were celebrating the nation's centennial across the country, and the Met was no different. According to museum historian Winifred Howe, in the spring of 1876, "a circular letter, signed by Parke Godwin, proposed a Centennial Summer Exhibition of New York's private collections of art, on the principle that New York ought to furnish to the many visitors of the centennial year more than its ordinary sources of entertainment, [and] the Museum was very ready to cooperate. In this exhibit the National Academy of Design united with the Museum; common committees were appointed; part of the pictures obtained - - 580 in number, from 58 contributors - were shown in the Museum and part in the Academy of Design…. During the 220 days approximately that the exhibition was open, from June 23rd to November 10th, the paying admissions amounted to 154,441…. To both institutions the financial help was very timely. …only about one-fourth of the paintings were the work of American artists and the remaining three-fourths were by modern European artists, English, French, and German."

At the same time, the Trustees continued to make progress toward building a new facility to house the museum's growing exhibits. In 1878, New York City passed an act giving $30,000 to be used for building the Central Park facility, and all the collections in the building were successfully moved by 1880. However, the first building was something of a disappointment; writing for *The New Yorker* in 2008, Macy Halford noted that Calvert Vaux, the lead architect on the project and one of Central Park's co-designers, "won the commission based on his standing as one of the masterminds of Central Park, but his initial museum building was declared, by its irascible president, 'a mistake.'" According to architectural historian Morrison Heckscher, "The new building opened to the public on March 30, 1880, to decidedly mixed reviews. The interiors generally met with approval, but the exterior suffered from being so obviously incomplete. From almost any angle the most striking elements were the raw, unfinished brick walls, intended one day to sprout additional wings."

An aerial picture of the Met's location in Central Park

Vaux

As if preparing the public for a look that would be disappointing, the Trustees' Annual Report of the previous year reminded its readers that "it must be borne in mind that it is part of a larger structure, and that every addition will tend to harmonize the whole edifice." Art critic James Jarves must not have read this caveat, for he called the building "a forcible example of architectural ugliness, out of harmony and keeping with its avowed purpose." He added that it was "fit only for a winter garden or a railway depot."

In his history of the building, Heckscher wrote, "Today,

although reroofed and entirely encased in later structures, portions of Vaux's building are still visible to the observant eye. In the Robert Wood Johnson Jr. Gallery, at the top of the Grand Staircase, part of one of the windows of the original Fifth Avenue facade is visible. The massive pointed arch of banded granite encloses a blind roundel, which stares out like a great cyclopean eye. In the Robert Lehman Wing, at the main-floor level, Vaux's entire west facade now forms the entrance wall. The narrow corridors at either side of the Grand Staircase lead through the original facade's windows into the Medieval tapestry hall, one of two sculpture galleries that opened directly onto the main hall…. Vaux's ceiling beams and molded cornices remain, although stripped of ornament. But what strikes the eye, because it retains the rich polychromy of the High Victorian Gothic, is the floor: a bold pattern of white and black marble, surrounded by narrow borders of red slate. On either side of the hall, enclosed stairways lead to the second-floor galleries. In 1880 these were the mostt-talked-about feature of the new building. When ascending the staircases, notable for their ample breadth and gentleness of ascent, one originally passed great circular windows that offered a view of almost the entire floor below…The staircases have recently been repainted to suggest their original polychrome glory. …
Photographs record the cheerful clutter of familiar landmarks at wildly disparate scale and also show the

great iron roof ribs with their quatrefoil openings. The original picture galleries were simply finished, revealing the strict economy required to complete the original building within budget."

It seems that at least some of those visiting the building wanted to like it, even as they found it difficult to do so. For instance, on April 30, 1880, the *New York Times* declared, "Modest, even sober in form and adornment, the Museum as it stands is a guarantee to the public who will have to pay, in the long run, for future additions-that the money has been so far carefully spent. It has gained, then, the confidence of the New Yorker of today, especially since he had been witness of so much rascality in the way of public expenditure in other places."

Nearly a decade after it was completed, Ripley Hitchcock, writing for Frank Wesley's *Popular Monthly*, observed that work was already underway to improve the look of the building: "This building was designed as merely a centre, a nucleus, but for ten years it stood naked and ashamed in all its dreary ugliness. The original plan…has not been adopted for the new wing which has been added to the southern side of the main building. The architecture has been termed a modified classic style, but there are arches over doors and windows, as well as pillars beside them, and the seemingly heavy roof, with its red cornice, is hardly to be classified. Perhaps it is safest to describe the architecture as composite, to overlook in congruities, and to recognize the vast improvement effected by the addition, as regards both the building and its relation to the Park landscape. From the southern front the ground falls away, and paths lead downward among the trees. A broad roadway curves around the building's front, from Fifth Avenue to the 'Eastern Drive,' which passes the western side of the Museum. Across this roadway is the Obelisk, 'Cleopatra's Needle,' so called, brought from Egypt by the munificence of the late W. H. Vanderbilt."

"Cleopatra's Needle" became one of the Met's most interesting objects, and entirely by chance. Six years before President Grover Cleveland dedicated the Statue of Liberty in 1886, a different monument that made its way to New York was an Ancient Egyptian obelisk from Alexandria that was nearly 3,000 years old. It took four months to move the monument from the harbor to Central Park, which was done through the use of a specially constructed railroad. The obelisk was then erected behind the Metropolitan Museum of Art, which holds millions of pieces of art but also partially obscures one of the oldest and most amazing pieces of art in the city. In October 1880, Freemasons held a full parade to dedicate the city's newest monument, which was known as "Cleopatra's Needle".

Pictures of Cleopatra's Needle

Cleopatra's Needle is one of the most unique artifacts in the city, and one of its most overlooked. Thousands of spectators attended the Freemasons' parade in 1880, but it's no longer high on people's lists of things to see in Central Park, let alone the rest of New York City. And to top it all off, the obelisk has nothing in common with the famous pharaoh it's named after.

About 3,500 years ago, an Egyptian pharaoh named Thutmose III ordered the construction of two identical 70 foot tall obelisks sculpted out of granite. He then had the obelisks inscribed with sets of hieroglyphics, and over the centuries other pharaohs had more inscriptions added, including the famous Biblical pharaoh Ramses II, who added new hieroglyphics praising Egyptian gods added as well. The obelisks remained at Heliopolis in Egypt for nearly 1,000 years until the Ancient Romans brought the obelisks to Alexandria, which had by then become the power center of Egypt. During the reign of Caesar Augustus, the Romans added crab statues to the bases of the obelisks in Alexandria for reasons that remain unknown, but these statues had symbols on them like a trowel, plummet, granite blocks and a white stone. These symbols had been cast in Roman cement, but the Freemasons believed that these symbols were Masonic emblems. In essence, they were connecting their fraternal order all the way back to Ancient Rome, and thus the elaborate procession to dedicate the monument.

At some point during Roman rule of Egypt, one of the obelisks fell over and lay in the sand for nearly 2,000 years, but the other continued to stand in place where the Romans left it. As a demonstration of their prestige and high culture, the British paid to have the obelisk still standing up transported to London in 1877, an idea they took from the French, who had already transported another Egyptian obelisk that was inscribed by Ramesses II to Paris in the 1820s. Egypt had long been part of the Ottoman Empire, but the imperialist European nations were expanding their influence in the region, and this left them in position to "purchase" the obelisks.

Just as the British copied the French, New Yorkers wanted to copy the British. Even though the British encountered deadly difficulty transporting the other "Cleopatra's Needle" obelisk to London, plans were made by tycoons across New York to transport its twin obelisk to New York City. William Vanderbilt donated $100,000 to get the obelisk, and city officials sent a request to Egypt's ruling official, the Khedive, asking to buy one of the obelisks. The Khedive assented in 1879 as a sign of goodwill to the United States, which had recently begun trading with Egypt after the opening of the Suez Canal.

Other than being an historic piece of art, on the surface Cleopatra's Needle doesn't seem to hold any special significance, but it was an important symbol to the city's inhabitants. The British and French had brought the obelisks to Paris and London to burnish the image of those cities as global power centers, and New York was following suit, ostensibly placing the importance of the city on the same pedestal as London and Paris. Bringing the obelisk to the city also demonstrated the growing cultural milieu and consciousness of the city. It may never attract as many visitors as the Statue of Liberty, but Cleopatra's Needle served as a symbol and reminder to the people who so desperately wanted it that New York City was one of the world's greatest cities.

The early 20th century guide also described Cleopatra's Needle: "It is an Egyptian monument of the 16th Century b. c, and was originally erected by Thothmes III before the Temple of the Sun in Heliopolis, near Cairo. Two hundred years later Rameses II, the Pharaoh of the Bible, added inscriptions to it setting forth his own achievements; and four centuries after another Pharaoh, Osarkon I, recorded his deeds along with those of Thothmes and Rameses. The center column of hieroglyphics on each face are those of Thothmes III. The sun-god Horus was symbolized by the sparrow hawk and this figure may be recognized at the top of each column. In 12 B. c. this obelisk and a companion one, now standing on the Thames Embankment, London, were removed to Alexandria by Augustus Caesar. The crabs at the base are reproductions of the bronze crabs which supported it during its sojourn in that city. Two of the originals are now in the Museum. In 1877 the Khedive of Egypt presented the obelisk to the United States, and in 1880 it was brought to New York. The obelisk is a granite monolith 69 feet in length and weighs 224 tons."

At the dedication of the monument, one speaker said, "This monument brings forcibly before us that period of which, at present, we know so little and of which the researches of the scholar, the calculation of the astronomer, the study of rocks and the skill of the engineer, are each year adding to our information and startling us with wonderful results. This trophy comes from that land the history of which was long lost in the mist of ancient fable and tradition — a land of wonderful creations of human power and genius — the birthplace of literature, the cradle of science and art and the people of those days excelled in many respects the advanced growth of the present century, etc. . . . Egyptians were the first to observe the course of the planets and regulate the year from the course of the sun. The pyramids were probably constructed not only to serve as tombs for some monarch but also designed for astronomical purposes — their position, exact angles as regards their situation and longitudinal lines, together with the peculiar entrances and the shadows cast into the interiors. Every stone and every line had some allusion to something yet to be accomplished and the exactness of calculations proves there was nothing accidental."

Around the same time all of that was going on, New Yorkers were still debating how to improve the museum and generate more interest. In 1881, the Met received its first bequest from Stephen Whitney Phoenix, a local who had inherited a significant fortune from his father. Phoenix devoted his life to studying and collecting antiquities, focusing much of his attention of portraits of founding members of the city. Upon his death, he left "his curiosities, works of art, pictures, and coins" to the museum, and among other things, his bequest formed the core of museum's substantial collection of Japanese art.

Phoenix's donation of art was obviously appreciated, but museums always need money, so when Levi Hale Willard bequeathed the Met $100,000 in 1883, the Trustees were ecstatic. The money was designated "for purchase of architectural casts," and while writing in the mid-20th century, journalist Joseph Noble described some of the objects bought with the money: "Greek, Roman, Egyptian, and Ancient Near Eastern statues and monuments comprised a large part of the collection, though important Romanesque, medieval and renaissance works were also well represented. The casts ranged in size from a kneeling Egyptian official only a few inches tall to a life-size reproduction of the entire facade of the Porch of the Maidens of the Erechtheum on the Athenian Acropolis. They were exhibited on the main floor of the building in Wings A, B, and C. According to the custom of the time, they were arranged not by period or provenance but almost entirely by size and shape. … The casts were studied not only by casual visitors…but also by students of art and design who used them for drawing exercises."

A. Balet's picture of Greek and Roman sculptures

A few years after the museum received these donations, it organized its first Departments of Paintings and Sculptures. It also received a bequest from William H. Vanderbilt, a member of one of New York's wealthiest families. In an 1891 report by Cesnola and Henry G. Marquand, the men insisted, "The most urgent demand, after provision for meeting the current expenses of the institution, is for an endowment fund, the income of which may be used for the purchase of rare and desirable art objects whenever they may be offered. At present our method of procedure, when such articles of value are offered, is to refer to the Trustees each case, with the question, "Shall a certain sum be subscribed for obtaining this object?" This involves delay, and generally ends in such lack of response that the matter goes by default. Experience has also shown this course to be impracticable for securing many articles brought to the notice of the Museum's officials. Over this slow and uncertain process, the superiority of a fund, the interest of which might be applied to the prompt acquisition of important things for sale, is obvious. The Museum would be in a position to improve many opportunities. Several fine objects have recently been lost to its collections in consequence of a want of ready money, or of inability to take prompt action."

The Vanderbilt bequest became the core of this fund, and it helped the museum purchase Egyptian art in 1886. Egyptology was all the rage in the late 19th century, and the collection would eventually number more than 25,000 pieces.

The following year brought the museum another massive gift. Catharine Lorillard Wolfe was a wealthy philanthropist and the only heir to her father's $12 million fortune (nearly $250 million today). In addition to funding projects for the Museum of Natural History and the

Newsboy's home, she spent huge sums of money amassing one of the most extensive art collections in the city, and when she died in 1887, she bequeathed her collection to the Met, forming the nucleus of the modern art collection. She also left the museum $200,000 in cash with which to house and expand the collection, leading to the building of the Catharine Lorillard Wolfe Wing. Unlike the many ancient pieces the museum already owned, the Wolfe collection appealed to the common man and attracted a new type of middle class clientele to the Met.

Wolfe

In most non-profit circles, money attracts money, and the Met was no different. A year after Wolfe's collection was installed, Marquand donated a collection of paintings by the Old Masters of Europe. Writing for the *Journal of Historians of Netherlandish Art*, Esmée Quodbach explained, "In December 1888, eager to show his recent

Old Master purchases to a larger audience, Marquand lent a group of thirty-seven works to the Metropolitan Museum, where they were exhibited in its new South Wing. The loan effected a sea change in the way New Yorkers—and, in a broader sense, Americans—were able to view art, as it introduced them directly to the works of some of the most celebrated Old Master painters, which until then only a fortunate few would have been able to see in person on their European travels." *The New York Times* agreed, adding, "Those who have seen the examples of Van Dyck, Rembrandt, Constable, Turner and other masters which are owned by Mr. Henry Marquand will appreciate the value of the opportunity offered by their public exhibition. These paintings…furnish an illustration of great art such as we have not had before. We trust that it may not be injudicious to express a hope that these superb paintings may remain at the Museum.' The following month, on January 10, 1889, Marquand gifted the museum with his collection, writing of his 'sincere pleasure' at how the exhibit had been received and adding that he was 'impressed that they would be of far greater service to the public to remain where they are, and in a public gallery, rather than in a private house."

Marquand

One of the Met's most famous paintings, Rembrandt's *Aristotle Contemplating the Bust of Homer* (1653)

Diego Velázquez's *Portrait of Juan de Pareja* (1650)

Rapid Expansion

As the museum's collections expanded, so did the building. In 1888, the museum added two new wings designed by Theodore Weston, with one on each side of the original building. According to Heckscher, Weston "chose to blend the two styles by means of tall, projecting pavilions. In their brick walls he inserted round-arched, three-part windows with massive pointed arches. For the roofs, he installed tall High Victorian mansards, complete with massive granite dormers—a…symbol of cosmopolitan modernity." There was also an "elevation identical to the executed south facade, except for a service entrance rather than a public one and windows in the second floor instead of panels for sculpture." Perhaps not surprisingly, the addition also had its detractors, with one critic complaining, "All who are familiar with the complete design of the late Wrey Mould must regret that it has been thrown aside to be replaced by the present squat and heavy structure."

For the rest of the century, and much of the next, donations continued to flow in. In 1889, writer Mary Elizabeth Adams Brown donated a collection of 270 musical instruments to the museum in memory of her husband, John Crosby Brown. The collection was one of the largest owned by any museum in the world, and Brown and her son continued to add to it in the decades that followed. This allowed the Met to use the $100,000 bequest it received from John Jacob Astor in 1890 to add to other departments and pay for building improvements. A year later, in 1891, Robert W. de Forest, long associated with the Wells Fargo Company, persuaded the museum to do a special fundraiser to purchase casts of important sculptures. He raised more than $78,000 that first year, and in the ones that followed, men like George Cullum of the American Geographical Society and John Taylor Johnston brought in more funds.

Brown

Shriram Rajagopalan's picture of one of Brown's gifts, a piano built by Bartolomeo Cristofori in 1720

**Another one of Brown's gifts, the Rectangular Octave
Virginal (built circa 1600)**

Jean-Christophe Benoist's picture of European sculptures in the Met

One thing that set the Met apart from the beginning was its curators' eyes for rising stars. In 1889, the museum acquired two paintings created by the recently deceased Impressionist, Edouard Manet. These would help bring attention to the museum's burgeoning collection of modern art, and they would be joined in the first decade of the 20ᵗʰ century by some of Auguste Renoir and Henri Matisse's paintings. In the case of Matisse, the Met was the first museum in the world to purchase his paintings.

Matisse's *The Young Sailor II* (1906), currently at the Met

The Met received another important bequest in 1891, when Edward C. Moore left the museum a sizeable collection of objects. According to information published by the Met in 1892, "Edward C. Moore was born in this city in 1827…. His father, John Moore, was a noted silversmith in his time, and Mr. Moore learned his craft…. [By 1851] the firm of John Moore & Co. was to manufacture silverware solely for Tiffany & Co., and in 1868 the entire plant owned by Mr. Moore was acquired by Tiffany and became a department in that business…There are in the collection specimens of antique Roman, Cyprian, Etruscan, Merovingian, Venetian, Persian and Arab. German and Spanish glass; Chinese and Japanese pottery; Hispano-Moresque, Rhodian, Damascus and Persian pottery ; Corean porcelain ; Chinese glass, jades and crystals : an unusual collection, both in number and quality, of Tanagra figurines ; Saracenic metal work of the twelfth and thirteenth centuries ; Persian, Turkish, Cashmere and Indian metal; Japanese and hinese bronzes, swords and sword guards ; inros and netsukis wood and ivory carvings, lacquers and Japanese basket work, Persian lacquer, Oriental jewelry, arid old French and Venetian inlaid straw work of 200 years ago. Besides all these objects there are included in the gift to the museum some 500 books on art, nearly all of them richly illustrated and some very rare…Perhaps the gem of the collection is in the cabinet of early Persian and Arab enamelled glass. It is a famous cup of slightly tinted buff glass, decorated in gold and blue and white enamel, with badges and an intricate pattern of conventionalized hounds, and an Arab distich in colored enamel. This is in fact a unique object, in that it is the earliest known dated specimen of Arabian glass. … In this same cabinet is a mosque lamp of archaic type of the thirteenth century, suspended by chains. It is of white glass with blue and white enamel inscription. Next in fame, artistic perfection, and exclusiveness to the enamelled cup is a large and beautiful vase of Arab glass with two handles and trumpet-shaped neck, and enamelled in colors. These mosque lamps are in form and decoration most perfect objects of Arabian glassware…"

In 1893, the museum opened a restaurant in the building, attracting wealthier New Yorkers and visitors from out of town who wanted to spend an entire day at the Met without having to leave in search of lunch. That same year, Elizabeth U. Coles, a wealthy widow, donated a collection of tapestries in memory of her dead son, William F. Coles. She also donated a substantial sum of money to the museum for the care and expansion of the collection.

With the collections growing so fast, the museum soon needed more room in which to house them. Fortunately, through the generous donations of patrons and organizations, the Met was able to open a new addition, this one designed by Arthur Tuckerman, in 1894, as well as another addition in 1902. According to a 2011 *Wall Street Journal* article, "The Museum's Beaux-Arts Fifth

Avenue facade and Great Hall, designed by the architect and founding Museum Trustee Richard Morris Hunt, opened to the public in December 1902. The Evening Post reported that at last New York had a neoclassical palace of art, 'one of the finest in the world, and the only public building in recent years which approaches in dignity and grandeur the museums of the old world.'"

Writing in 1904, the famous author Henry James praised the building, describing it as "a palace of art, truly, that sits there on the edge of the Park, rearing itself with a radiance. . . . It spoke with a hundred voices of that huge process of historic waste that the place in general keeps putting before you; but showing it in a light that drew out the harshness or the sadness, the pang, whatever it had seemed elsewhere, of the reiterated sacrifice to pecuniary profit. For the question here was to be of the advantage to the spirit, not the pocket; to be of the aesthetic advantage involved in the wonderful clearance to come."

With the museum itself now complete, the Trustees were able to turn their attention more fully back to the collections. Thus, the early years of the 20th century saw the museum acquire a large collection of jade, along with a collection of Boscoreale frescoes and a bronze biga, a two horse chariot from the Etruscan era. The 2011 *Wall Street Journal* article explained, "By the twentieth century, the Museum had become one of the world's great art centers. In 1907, the Museum acquired a work by Auguste Renoir, and in 1910, the Met was the first public institution in the world to acquire a work of art by Henri Matisse. The ancient Egyptian hippopotamus statuette that is now the Museum's unofficial mascot, 'William,' entered the collection in 1917. Today, virtually all of the Museum's thirty-six thousand ancient Egyptian objects, the largest collection of Egyptian art outside of Cairo, are on display."

The Met made another leap forward in the early 20th Century when in created an Education Department to reach out to local schools and open up its doors to children, and to encourage teachers to visit the museum with their classes. The 1908 addition to the museum created enough space so that a room could be set aside for the museum's first classroom, a place where those among the youngest citizens of the city could meet to learn more about art and culture. The Met took this process one step further the following year when it hired its first Museum Instructor.

These actions were all part of a plan established in 1907 to expand the museum's influence into New York classrooms. According the one report from that year, "Special written information will be given at any time to teachers who will designate in advance the work which they wish to illustrate. A class room with seating capacity of about one hundred and fifty to two hundred and containing apparatus for stereopticon exhibition, has been set aside for the use of teachers with pupils and may be secured at any time during Museum hours, notice being given in advance in order to prevent conflicting visits. When the visits of teachers or pupils fall on 'pay days/'provision is made for their admission without charge. Photographs and lantern slides from the collections of the Museum are sent to the class room when desired, and assistance in selecting those which will be of use in the ground to be covered by the teacher's lecture is gladly given. Direct intercourse between the Museum and the teachers is had from time to time, and lectures on special subjects are being given by members of the Museum staff…The Museum holds itself ready at all times to confer with teachers and to assist as far as it may in their work, and it is hoped that in the future they will find it possible to take more advantage of the benefits which the institution can give than the demands of the school system have seemed to permit in the past." For those who could not make it to the museum, the Met also created a lending library of "lantern slides," ancestors to the Kodak slides from the 1970s. These slides featured excellent black and white photographs of pieces in the museum's collection, and were made available to school and civic groups, along with descriptive brochures that would allow a speaker to present an educational and entertaining program.

The 1908 addition brought other changes to the museum, as the architects, McKim, Mead & White, detailed in a report: "In undertaking the development of the general plan, it was our aim, first, to secure an arrangement of buildings and courts, of galleries and corridors, which should provide ample exhibition spaces, abundant light, free circulation and units of dimensions so flexible as to permit of the utmost freedom in the future development of individual parts. Architecturally we sought to establish a scale which would give a proper sense of proportion and dignity to the building which was intended to house the greatest museum of fine arts in America, and which from its purpose, its setting, and its very dimensions was destined to be the most important public edifice in New York."

One aspect that set Charles McKim, the firm's architectural expert, apart from many of the museum's earlier designers was his appreciation of light and its importance in illuminating and framing artwork. While later conservators might curse his plans, the public marveled at the beauty his designed revealed, which featured light colored walls and a tall central hall that reached 6 stories and had "ten large semicircular clerestory windows." These windows proved to be the most stunning feature of the new addition, and one author described the effects: "These give to the hall a high side light which is beautifully diffused by the cream-white, vaulted ceiling, and falls most becomingly upon the sculptures and other objects on the floor and walls below. The shadows cast by it are never too sharp, and it is equally good in all parts of the hall. To prevent reflection and inversed shadows from the floor, it was necessary to use material of a neutral tone, and for this Tennessee marble with an unpolished surface was successfully adopted."

McKim

The Met also placed an Information Desk in a prominent location at the front of the museum, again making the facility more welcoming and open to common people. Among the topics those staffing the desk were likely to be asked about in the early 1900s was Egypt. Wars in that area had resulted in many antiquities being removed from the country, leading to a craze for all things Egyptian. As such, in a bid to attract both new visitors and new donors, the museum organized a Department of Egyptian Art in 1906 and began to plan its own Egyptian Expedition. In its 1911 "Handbook to the Egyptian Rooms," the museum explained, "The galleries of the Egyptian Department…have been undergoing a gradual process of rearrangement during the past few years and three new rooms have been added to the series since the department was opened to the public in 1911. This rearrangement and expansion of the collection have been due to the additional material which is being received year by year from the work of the Museum's Expedition in Egypt and, in the near future, two more rooms are to be added to the series and further changes in the arrangement of the collection are to be made."

Of course, there was much more to the museum than just its Egyptian collection. During this period, George A. Hearn donated paintings from the European and American traditions, while insisting that they all be displayed together, as they had been while on loan. "The fifty-one paintings in this collection in Gallery 15 embrace only four nationalities, 34 of them being English, 8 Dutch and Flemish, 3 French and 6 American. … The Americans were purposely hung in the Gallery to show that good American pictures can hold their own against the foreigners; I never having discriminated in making purchases, the test always being, 'Is the picture good?' and the only preference being to buy the American when quality and value were equal."

This presented something of a challenge to the museum, since its practice at that time was to display art in chronological order throughout the facility. He finally struck a deal with the museum that the paintings would remain together for 25 years before being separated, and that he would donate a total of $150,000 to the Met to be invested so that the proceeds could be used in the future to purchase more pieces by American artists. He also donated more paintings to the collection in 1910.

The early 1900s were a prosperous time for America and the Met, as men who had made their fortunes during the late 19th century industrial boom began to sit back and enjoy their money. In 1908, wealthy philanthropist Frederick C. Hewitt gave the museum $1.5 million, and John Steward Kennedy gave $2.6 million. Among other improvements, these donations and others like them allowed the Met to open its first Study Room, this one for the purpose of allowing visitors a closer look at textiles. This was a good choice, as many wealthy women of the era were fascinated by fancy needlework and came to the museum to study techniques. The museum also opened a Decorative Arts Wing, which was obviously quite attractive to those whose taste in art ran toward home furnishings more than classical paintings.

More additions and renovations followed, including the museum's first library in 1910 and its Lecture Hall in 1911. The former, according to one museum report from the era, "should be a storehouse of information upon any subject illustrated by the Museum collections -- irrespective of the fact that the same or similar books are to be found upon the shelves of other City Libraries in order that the necessary sources of information may be open and easy of access to the Directors and Curators of the Museum and also to all of its visitors who are students and not simply sightseers…the acquisition of fine and rare books would appear to be within the province of a Library of Art. Monuments of early printing, illuminated manuscripts, and book bindings from the hands of renowned bibliopegists of former times are as much works of art...as paintings on canvas or sculptures in stone, and as full of the inspiration that flows only from original works of art."

In 1911, Francis L. Leland, whom the *New York Times* called a "Most Liberal Living Donor," gave the museum more than a million dollars, much of which went to build and outfit yet another addition by McKim, Mead & White in 1913. Writing in 1941, Winifred Howe recalled, "Two events determined the use of most of the twenty-four rooms in this latest wing. …J. P. Morgan was very eager, for the benefit of the public, to have his father's superb collection, then in the Museum, placed on exhibition at the earliest possible moment. The second floor of Wing H, already planned for another installation but not yet in use, was gladly assigned to hold the Morgan collection, and a loan exhibition of it was opened in February 1914. The event that decided the installation of most of the first-floor galleries was equally happy. In May 1913 William Henry Riggs of Paris, a lifelong friend of the late J. Pierpont Morgan, gave to the museum his superb collection of arms and armor. Fortunately the new wing with its impressive central court was well adapted to show this great gift…"

Arad's picture of the collection of arms and armor in the Met

As Howe noted, Morgan did not live to see this installation, but he had left the museum a giant fortune in art and money. In the first *History of the Museum*, published in 1913, Howe noted, "Mr. Morgan brought to the service of the Museum an earnest zeal for its welfare and an intimate acquaintance with the world of art in all its branches, coupled with every quality of leadership. His intuitive perception, his quick and decisive action, joined to his broad knowledge of men and affairs and his powerful influence, have combined to make that leadership singularly effective."

Morgan would no doubt have been pleased with the direction his legacy took in the years following his death, for one bequest followed another, including funding to properly display the Museum's Egyptian Expedition's findings, as well as the newly gifted Tomb of Pernab, a gift of English furniture and bric-a-brac from politician John L. Cadwalader, paintings, tapestries, and, of course, more money, totaling more than $5.5 million in bequests alone by 1920. Morgan's son, no doubt touched by his father's devotion to the museum and hoping to burnish his family's legacy, donated the legendary Renaissance artist Raphael's Colonna altarpiece. J.P. Morgan, Jr. also donated a French sculpture in 1915, and other objects that would fill the Pierpont Morgan Wing of Decorative Arts in 1918.

J.P. Morgan and J.P. Morgan, Jr.

Rolf Müller's picture of the entrance to the Tomb of Pernab at the Met

Though it is unlikely that anyone realized it at the time, the Met in 1917 acquired a statue that would eventually become the most famous and easily recognized piece in its collection. According to the museum's own website, the hippopotamus, dating from the 12th Egyptian Dynasty and standing only 4 ½ inches tall, was given to the Met by Edward Harkness, a popular American philanthropist. The website notes, "This well-formed statuette of a hippopotamus…demonstrates the Egyptian artist's appreciation for the natural world. It was molded in faience, a ceramic material made of ground quartz. Beneath the blue glaze, the body was painted with the outlines of river plants, symbolizing the marshes in which the animal lived. … To the ancient Egyptians, the hippopotamus was one of the most dangerous animals in their world. The huge creatures were a hazard for small fishing boats and other rivercraft. … This example was one of a pair found in a shaft associated with the tomb chapel of the steward Senbi II at Meir, an Upper Egyptian site about thirty miles south of modern Asyut. Three of its legs have been restored because they were probably purposely broken to prevent the creature from harming the deceased."

**William the Hippopotamus, an Egyptian statue
dating back to about 1900 BCE**

The article concludes, "The hippo's modern nickname
first appeared in 1931 in a story that was published in the
British humor magazine Punch. It reports about a family
that consults a color print of the Met's hippo—which it
calls 'William'—as an oracle. The Met republished the
story the same year in the Museum's Bulletin, and the
name William caught on!" Today, William the Hippo
serves as the museum's unofficial mascot and is beloved
by the museum's staff and visitors.

The museum closed out the 1910s by instituting their

first in an ongoing series of free concerts, offered to the public on the museum's grounds and attracting both stellar artists and large crowds of appreciative listeners. At the same time, the museum was experiencing an interest in European art unlike any it had ever known before; the Great War had taken thousands of Americans across the sea and exposed them to European culture in a way that had been unknown to their relatives. Many came back and headed to the Met, anxious to see items of similar quality as those they had seen across the Atlantic.

The 1920s proved to be a period of steady but unremarkable growth, as the Met continued to add to its collections. One of the biggest challenges facing the museum during this period was how to balance the needs and wants of the rising business and middle classes with the Met's tradition of sophistication and culture. Gone were the wealthy philanthropists who began to see philanthropy as both a mission and a way to enhance their legacies; conversely, business leaders in the 1920s were more aggressive and constantly in search of a new product to produce and market. Writing for *The New Yorker* in 1925, Murdock Pemberton complained about the role of Richard Bach, who was appointed to work with manufacturers to make items from the museum's collection available to these manufacturers. Pemberton wrote, "You may jump to the conclusion that something from an Egyptian queen's hand might [interest] the jewelers and no one else. And that would show that you don't know anything more about it than we do. Mr. Bach is earnest about it. Copying is no good. In fact, he altogether leave out of his plans the individuals or firms who merely see the Museum as a place where beautiful things are on view to be copied. They come and go unmolested, and are helped only when they seek help. Design, to Bach, is not static. It is living and should be adapted to this day and this period…Take for instance the textile people. Came a man who had read about King Tut. Great, says he, let's have a line of King Tut silks. Mr. Bach shook his head sadly and tried to explain that it wouldn't do. The idea wasn't sould design. The adornments to King Tut's tomb were architectonic; they would be out of place in a lady's dress. Now we do have some very fine scarved that the Queen's maids wore; they might suggest something in the way of design that would better suit the medium. But the business man had read the paper and he knew a front page story. He insisted. So Mr. Bach pointed the way to the Eqyptian room and said, go ahead, it's a fad and can't last five months. Mr. Bach smiles when he recalles that exactly five months to the day the silk man called and asked if Mr. Bach could suggest any way to utilize or reprint about a half million dollars worth of King Tut Novelty Fabrics!"

Recent History

The 1930s brought new challenges in the form of a distinct slowdown in donations and paid visitors, byproducts of the Great Depression, which affected every aspect of life in America. However, even as the museum appeared to be at something of a standstill during this era, the Trustees were laying the groundwork to expand into a new and fascinating facility. Those strolling along Fort Washington Avenue in Manhattan were the first to notice something was going on in the mid-1930s. Writing in 1979, museum historian Bonnie Young explained, "The initial imagination was that of the American sculptor George Grey Barnard. Before 1914, when he lived in France, Barnard collected much of the architectural material seen in The Cloisters today, including the columns and capitals of the Saint-Guilhem, Cuxa, Bonnefont, and Trie cloisters. Barnard's accomplishment in exhibiting this material in a special building on Fort Washington Avenue, not far from The Cloisters' site, was recognized when he put the collection up for sale in the 1920s. …in 1925…John D. Rockefeller, Jr., donated funds to The Metropolitan Museum of Art for the purchase and continued exhibition of the collection, to which he added some forty medieval sculptures from his own collection. Subsequently, when Rockefeller presented to New York City the land that became Fort Tryon Park, he reserved the northern hilltop for the construction of a larger and better-developed museum of medieval art."

She added, "The design for this structure was entrusted to Charles Collens, the architect of the Riverside Church in New York. Collens' first consultant in the planning was Joseph Breck…. Upon Breck' death in 1933, the responsibility passed to his colleague James J. Rorimer. Collens and Rorimer, architect and curator, worked closely together throughout the construction period, and more than any others, determined the final form of the building…After four years of construction beginning in 1934, The Cloisters opened in 1938. It is not a copy of any particular medieval structure, but an ensemble of rooms and gardens that suggest, rather than duplicate, the European originals. The rooms and halls and chapels of the main floor are built around the largest of the four cloisters, the one from Saint-Michel-de-Cuxa. On the lower floor, which is served by two stairways, are the Gothic Chapel, the walls of which rise the height of the two floors, and two garden cloisters, the Bonnefont and the Trie. On the lower floor, too, will be found the Glass Gallery and the Treasury, which house objects not closely connected with any of The Cloisters' architectural settings."

Pawel Drozd's picture of the Cloisters

Much of the latter half of the 20th century saw the Met fall into something of a rut. The museum remained opened throughout World War II, but its importance was badly overshadowed by international concerns. The post-war period of the 1950s saw yet another boon for the American economy and a rise in the middle-class, but the museum continued to pursue its mission of expanding the nation's sense of art and culture. According to author Jeffery Trask, " [The] postwar museum followed the cultural politics of postindustrial cities. Museums tried to lure their audiences from the suburbs, cloaking themselves in the mantel of cultural authority. In fact, once New York became the cultural capital of the world, and modern art and design became symbols of urbanity and intellectual sophistication, art museums in cities stood as symbols of cultural distinction. In increasingly abandoned downtown districts, an urban art museum represented one of the few draws to sustain the urban economy. With fewer tax dollars to support municipal institutions, museums and libraries curtailed outreach programs. The combined factors of the economic decline that followed deindustrialization and shrinking tax revenues, which contributed to the white flight of middle-class Americans to suburban communities, also contributed to images of racially divided inner cities…To entice suburban visitors to make trips into the city, art museums revived ideas about the refining influences of art that a generation of museum reformers in the early twentieth century had worked so hard to overturn. Rather than focus on inner-city communities…the museums in industrial cities like Cleveland and Detroit used their limited resources and energy to attract traditional museum visitors, who already had the cultural knowledge to appreciate art, to come into the city for the day. So successfully did subsequent generations of leaders in museums and other cultural institutions obscure the legacy of progressive connoisseurs that public and institutional memory has lost sight of the democratic ideas they promoted as they sought to make museums public institutions in the service of the people."

It was amidst this social climate that the Met received a

mysterious donation of $4.5 million. According to an *Associated Press* article from December 1958, the museum "had no advance knowledge of the bequest—one of the largest sums ever left to a museum—made by an Upstate woman whose contacts with the Metropolitan had been few." The donor was Mrs. Thomas H. Foulds, who had recently died at the age of 94, and in many ways she and her husband represented the type of patron the museum was attracting during the 20th century. According to the article, "Mrs. Foulds, whose late husband was a dentist, inherited her fortune from her father, Jeremiah T. Finch, one of the founders of a paper manufacturing and lumber concern…. In 1921, Mrs. Foulds' husband became a Fellow for Life of the Metropolitan Museum of Art with a contribution of $1,000. His wife followed suit in 1925. Shortly before these contributions were made, the couple traveled to Egypt and was in touch with an archeological expedition from the Museum. Interested in the work, the couple contributed $3,000 for Egyptian purchases. Following Dr. Foulds' death in 1931, Mrs. Foulds gave a tankard to the museum. That was the last the museum heard from her until Thursday."

The museum enjoyed a brief return to the spotlight during the short years of the Kennedy administration thanks to First Lady Jacqueline Kennedy. Long a devotee of art and culture, she encouraged and supported its efforts to expand, but the assassination of President John F. Kennedy brought this period to an abrupt and violent end, and over the course of the 1960s, the middle class ceded much of its influence to a younger generation that rebelled against much of the beauty that the Met offered. Modern art took on a chaotic and dark feel that many on the board were reluctant to embrace. Even as pressure came from above to focus on the institution's classical collection, pressure pushed up from below demanding that the Met expand its holdings to embrace the newer trends in art. This tension continued throughout the 1970s and was only resolved over time by the fact that those who had put together the museum's collections before World War II aged and died, and responsibilities fell to the younger, more progressive generations.

That is not to say that all the museum's challenges disappeared, for the 1980s saw a new rise in conservative thought in the United States, and once more, the Met was an easy focal point for people on both the right and the left to fight their battles. On more than one occasion, members of traditional religious groups complained about displays that they considered blasphemous, and some even pressured the National Endowment for the Arts, formed by the federal government in 1965 to provide "funding and support [to give] Americans the opportunity to participate in the arts, exercise their imaginations, and develop their creative capacities," to pull its funding from the museum. These controversies likely benefitted the museum more than they harmed it, given that there's no such thing as bad publicity.

While the Met's collection was in flux during these years, the building was expanding at a slow, but steady pace, in keeping with an architectural plan created by Kevin Roche, John Dinkeloo & Associates in 1971 "to make the Museum's collections more accessible to the public, more useful to the scholars and, in general, more interesting and informative to all visitors." A number of additions opened during these years, including the Robert Lehman Wing in 1975. Dedicated to the Old Masters, Impressionist, and Post-Impressionist paintings that made the museum famous, it anchored the museum to its past. In the years that followed the wing's opening, the Met expanded its collection to include 5 of the 35 extant paintings created by Johannes Vermeer. These, along with more than 2,500 other European paintings, make the Met's collection one of the largest in the world.

Sumanch's picture of the Robert Lehman Wing

Johannes Vermeer's *Woman with a Lute* (1662), one of his paintings housed at the Met

The Sackler Wing opened to the public in 1978 as the home for the Temple of Dendur from Egypt and soon became a popular site for families to visit. In the decades that followed, the museum expanded its display in this wing to include most of the Egyptian items in its collections, more than 25,000 in all. To see a larger display of Egyptian art objects, visitors would have to travel to Cairo itself.

Jean-Christophe Benoist's picture of the Temple of Dendur

Building on the interest in American history stirred up by the bicentennial celebrations in 1976, the American Wing opened in 1980 to display 25 different rooms, each designed to represent a particular time and place in the history of the United States. Work would continue on this wing well into the 21st century before it was finally completed in 2012. Today there is no larger collection of American sculptures, paintings, or decorative arts anywhere else in the world.

One of America's most famous paintings, *Washington Crossing the Delaware* by Emanuel Leutze, at the Met

In keeping with his family's tradition of supporting the Met, Michael C. Rockefeller donated the funding for the wing that would bear his name. It opened in 1982 and housed much of the museum's collection of items from Africa and Oceania, as well as North America and South America. His donation inspired others, and in 1987, the museum opened the Lile Acheson Wallace Wing, which houses contemporary art. Also in 1987, the *New York Times* reported, "A gift of $10 million has been pledged to the Metropolitan Museum of Art by Milton J. Petrie, chairman of the Petrie Stores Corporation, a chain of retail stores specializing in women's apparel. The money will be used for a sculpture court in the four-story wing being built to house European sculpture and decorative arts. The $51 million wing, the final element in the Met's master plan of 1970, will fill the last gap in the museum's western facade." Speaking on behalf of the museum, Arthur Sulzberger, chairman of the Met's Board of Trustees, gushed, "This major gift guarantees the museum's ability to build a very important new space, one that will beautifully connect a number of sections of the museum to one another…"

The article continued, "The Carroll and Milton Petrie European Sculpture Court, facing Central Park, is to be 32 feet wide by 240 feet long. A pyramidal skylight is to rise 63 feet at its highest point. Cited by Philippe de Montebello, the Met's director, as "the last vast open space within the museum," it has been designed to evoke a formal French garden of the period of Louis XIV. It will provide…a noble setting for monumental European statuary of the 17th, 18th and 19th centuries from the Met's substantial collection. Additional works will be shown in an arcade along the court's south side. As part of the project, the museum's former carriage entrance, on the north side of the court, is to be restored to its original 16th-century Italian Revival style. This facade, designed by Theodore Weston with Arthur Tuckerman, was completed in 1888. Mr. Petrie's gift matches the $10 million given last June by Laurence A. Tisch, chairman and president of the Loews Corporation and chief executive of CBS Inc., and his brother, Preston R. Tisch, Postmaster General of the United States. Their donation will go toward the building of special exhibition galleries in the new wing…"

A few years later, Henry R. Kravis donated funding for yet another wing, this one devoted to showcasing the Met's collection of traditional European sculptures and decorative pieces dating from the Renaissance to the end of the 19th century.

The museum completed its expansion program in 1991, but it has continued to build and develop its collection, bringing a more international feel into the museum with the addition in 1998 of the Arts of Korea Gallery, which made up an entire suite of rooms devoted to Asian art. . The Ancient Near Eastern Art galleries reopened a year later in 1999.

On February 24, 2004, the *Associated Press* reported on another expansion project: "The Metropolitan Museum of Art today announced plans to launch—and fund—a series of milestone 21st-Century Met interior construction projects aimed at dramatically enhancing the Museum's displays of Hellenistic and Roman art, Etruscan art, Islamic art, 19th-century art, modern art, and modern photography. Additionally, the major new 'building-from-within' program will substantially upgrade the Museum's Ruth and Harold D. Uris Center for Education, the traditional welcoming point of entry for some 125,000 school visitors each year. To finance the projects, the Museum announced a new plan to complete private funding for the construction and rehabilitation work. … Under the comprehensive plans unveiled today, [Museum Director Philippe] de Montebello announced, [the Museum Restaurant] will now be overhauled and converted back to gallery space so that the Met's vast collection of classical art…can again be displayed here in a new Leon Levy and Shelby White Court for Roman and Etruscan Art and surrounding galleries."

In describing the plans, de Montebello himself explained, "Determined never to become a museum of itself, yet at the same time cognizant of its longtime commitment to undertake no expansion beyond its current footprint, the Metropolitan is charting a future based on the best possible use of its magnificent interior spaces in the fullest service of its collections and its public. The new galleries that will be built from within will reopen to visitors some of the most majestic spaces in its landmark building, and, of vast significance, permit the institution's outstanding collection of Hellenistic, Roman, and Etruscan art—long in storage—to return at last to public view in breathtaking new galleries. At the same time, the renewal work we plan to undertake immediately below the new Roman Court will create a suitably inspiring gateway to the Museum for its youngest visitors—the museum-going public of the future—namely, the students and school groups from throughout our City and region whose proper, stimulating introduction to great art we take as a crucial aspect of our Museum mission…With the reinstallation of the Hellenistic, Etruscan, and Roman collection, and the construction of new and improved space for the display of Islamic art, 19th-century art, modern art, and modern photography, the 21st-Century Met will be able to present, more comprehensively and more authoritatively, its encyclopedic collections of art from 5,000 years of human creativity."

Vice Chairman of the Metropolitan E. John Rosenwald, Jr. added, "This new phase of our capital campaign reflects the urgency of these construction and endowment projects. There is a critical need to enhance our facilities in order to best serve our many audiences and continue to fulfill our mission to educate and to inspire, all at the very highest levels. With great appreciation of our past donors, we look forward to these new challenges with enthusiasm and optimism."

Addressing concerns about the impact the construction project would have on the city and the surrounding area,

David McKinney, the Met's president, assured the public, "The Museum will of course continue to work closely with our public officials, with City Hall and the Governor's Office, with the City Council and State Legislature, and with representatives of the surrounding community, to provide efficient, reliable, and continuous communication to them and to our public as these projects move forward. The generous support we have received from government at all levels has been invaluable to us, and we pledge, as always, to provide our constituencies with the levels of service and space they have come to expect from the Met."

The museum's first goal in these renovations was to replace the restaurant with the Leon Levy and Shelby White Court for Roman and Etruscan Art. The article explained, "For half a century, the Museum has been using this vast gallery—designed and originally used to exhibit Roman art—for other purposes. In 1950, the Museum converted the space in the southeast corner of the building into a public restaurant, to which a cafeteria was later added. The Museum closed this facility in June 2003, relocating its kitchen facilities and opening a highly popular new public cafeteria…. This…has liberated the old restaurant space for its long-planned and widely anticipated conversion back to a gallery for Hellenistic and Roman art…. Leading to the current construction phase, the Metropolitan opened its widely praised constellation of galleries for classical art beginning eight years ago: Cycladic and early Greek art galleries in 1996, and its new Greek and Cypriot art galleries in 1999 and 2000, respectively."

The museum also made plans to refurbish the Ruth and Harold D. Uris Center For Education, beloved and remembered by thousands as their first introduction to the Met. The plan called for the museum to enlarge and update the area to make it more accessible for school groups and disabled visitors.

With all these changes, de Montebello insisted, the museum would maintain its cultural integrity: "Just as the Great Hall, designed by Richard Morris Hunt more than a century ago, inspires wonder and expectation the public spaces at 81st Street will also convey the dignity and distinction of The Metropolitan Museum of Art. For all visitors have a right to encounter our collections and exhibitions in the most inspiring manner, and deserve to be honored by their visit."

The museum made excellent progress with these plans, as the board reported in 2005: "The Museum continued to make major progress on its "21st Century Met" construction program and also entered the final stage of its four-year project to renovate the facade. Capital expenditures amounted to $61.4 million, of which…over half, were related to the construction of the new Leon Levy and Shelby White Court for Roman and Etruscan art and the renovation of the Ruth and Harold D. Uris Center for Education and related projects. Another $3.4 million was spent on the 19thCentury Galleries expansion, which will provide an additional 9,000 square feet of space to showcase works from the late nineteenth century and early twentieth century."

As anyone who has ever renovated a house knows, there's always more work to do, and so it was with the Met. As the museum was making all the slated changes, its leaders made plans to improve the galleries that adjoined the new White Court. The goal of these changes were "to present, in adjacent spaces, as well as in galleries one flight above, a substantial number of works from the Museum's rich collection of Hellenistic art, and the arts of South Italy and Sicily, whose display will provide a vital artistic and historical link between the Greek and the new Roman galleries." Among their other features, the gallery would showcase a Hellenistic Treasury built just outside the new Roman Court.

This movement represented a change in focus for the museum, giving visitors the opportunity "to view these masterpieces in the proper context of sculpture, bronzes, and other arts of the late Hellenistic and early Roman periods." Such was its commitment to this goal that the Met even sacrificed some of its executive office space to expand the area.

As much as institutions like the Met prefer to remain politically neutral, they must at all times be sensitive to the political climate in which they are operating. This can be a problem when long term plans are drawn up and then must be implemented in a different context, and never was this so awkward as when part of the Met's 21st century updates called for its Islamic Art galleries to be closed for renovation soon after 9/11 devastated New York City. De Montebello admitted, "Given the current geopolitical situation, and the increased interest in Islamic art, this is an unfortunate moment to announce the temporary closing of the Met's Islamic Galleries. But I am extremely proud that so many of the finest works from this department will remain on view—either on the Great Hall balcony or imbricated throughout the Museum in the galleries of other curatorial departments."

Fortunately, the renovation went well, and it proved to be worth the wait when it reopened in 2012. Writing for the *Washington Report on Middle East Affairs*, Elaine Pasquini observed, "The museum's former Islamic gallery reopened Nov. 1, renamed the Galleries for the Art of the Arab Lands, Turkey, Iran, Central Asia, and Later South Asia. That these priceless treasures from the Islamic world re-emerged in 2011-the year of the Arab Spring which brought hope, as well as an unknown future, to regions which produced some of these works-has not gone unnoticed and is a subject of animated discussion among lovers of Islamic art. Some 1,200 exquisite items of ceramics, carpets, textiles, jewelry, glassware, sculptures, metalwork, calligraphy and paintings from the museum's 12,000-piece collection-one of the world's most extensive-are now presented chronologically in 15 galleries covering 19,000 square feet, providing visitors with a more rewarding museum experience." Marika Sardar, a research associate with the museum, agreed, adding, "These items are all displayed in these galleries because they are connected by Islamic culture. The objects are from regions that were either ruled by Muslims, or had a majority population that were Muslim. The art is not always religious in nature, but is connected by this common culture."

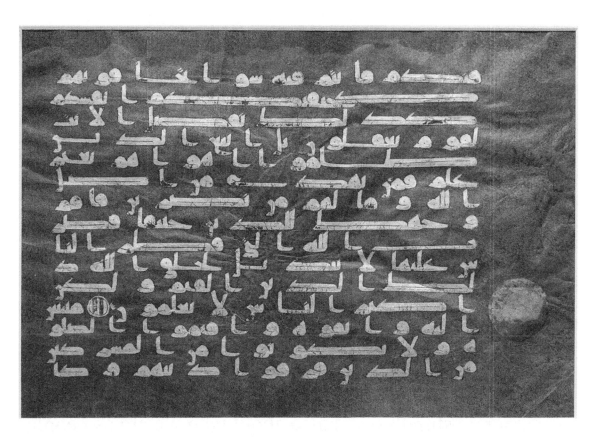

Marie-Lan Nguyen's picture of a Leaf from the Blue Qur'an in the Met

As part of its ongoing plan of "building from within," the museum added about 9,000 square feet of exhibit space devoted to showcasing examples of modern photography, as well as other modern art pieces and items from the 19th century. It also began work on the American Wing in the hopes of returning a large number of pieces from its American collection to public view. First Lady Michelle Obama was on hand for the reopening of the gallery and told those present, "I am delighted to be here with you to celebrate American history through the arts. From the beginning of our nation, the inspired works of our artists and artisans have reflected the ingenuity, creativity, independence and beauty of this nation. It is the painter, the potter, the weaver, the silversmith, the architect, the designer whose work continues to create an identity for America that is respected and recognized around the world as distinctive and new. … Our future as an innovative country depends on ensuring that everyone has access to the arts and to cultural opportunity. Nearly 6 million people make their living in the non-profit arts industry, and arts and cultural activities contribute more than $160 billion to our economy every year. … The intersection of arts and commerce is about more than economic stimulus, it's also about who we are as people."

The pieces included everything from paintings and sculptures to silver and ceramics. The plan also called for significant improvements in the way the public was able to move through the galleries. "The result," according to journalist Leo O'Donovan, "is a place full of light and wonder--a thirty-thousand-square-foot exhibition space you can wander through without losing your way…Everything now resides on a single floor--the second--a lovely simplification achieved by literally raising the roof at the far western wall of the museum. The design can be seen as minimalism's tribute to the Beaux Arts style of the buildings for which much of this art was originally acquired. The walls are painted in a specially designed off-white or oyster, the flooring is white oak; each painting is spot-lit, while the overall wall-wash lighting is computer-adjusted to change with the daylight that pours into the many skylighted galleries. This lets drama arise from the art itself, and from how you choose to approach it--either along broad chronological lines, following several main axes that cut through the various galleries, or with attention to special themes."

On March 18, 2016, the Met opened the latest addition to its ever-expanding number of buildings, leasing a large building on Madison Avenue. The Met-Breuer "enables visitors to engage with the art of the 20th and 21st centuries through the global breadth and historical reach of The Met's unparalleled collection and resources through a range of exhibitions, commissions, performances, and artist residencies." The *Associated Press* reported, "The new space…is housed in the Marcel Breuer-designed building that was the longtime home of the Whitney Museum of American Art, before it move downtown last year. The restored Bauhaus-style building…[gives]the met 29,000-square-feet of space for displaying and expanding its 12,000-work collection of 20th and 21st century art."

Professor of Museum Studies Bruce Alshuler, of New York University, praised the opening exhibit, "Unfinished: Thoughts Left Visible," as "a perfect example of what they can do that other museum are unlikely and certainly cannot do to the depth that the Met can." He added that the Met was "playing to its strong suit, which is a unique positioning, to create that kind of exhibition." The museum's Head of Modern and Contemporary Art emphasized the importance of having continuity across all of the museum's exhibits, saying, "We can tell stories that reach far beyond the 1900 boundary back to any point within the huge span of five millenniums of art represented by the Met. At the Met, we hope history and art will have a natural companionship."

Like the art it houses, the Met has changed with the times. Beginning as a place to show the world that America was not a cultural backwater, it has become one of the most prominent art museums in the world. In one place, anyone, from children to retirees, can experience the wonder of humankind's creative spirit from the beginning of recorded history to the present day. As long as people keep creating art, the Met will be there to preserve it.

Online Resources

Other books about art history by Charles River Editors

Other books about French history by Charles River Editors

Other books about the Louvre on Amazon

Other books about the Met on Amazon

Further Reading

Bierman, Irene A (2003). *Napoleon in Egypt*. Ithaca Press.

Danziger, Danny (2007). Museum: Behind the Scenes at the Metropolitan Museum of Art. Viking, New York City.

Edwards, Henry Sutherland (1893). *Old and New Paris: Its History, Its People, and Its Places*. Paris: Cassell and Co. Retrieved 30 April 2008.

Howe, Winifred E., and Henry Watson Kent (2009). A History of the Metropolitan Museum of Art. Vol. 1. General Books, Memphis.

McClellan, Andrew (1999). *Inventing the Louvre: Art, Politics, and the Origins of the Modern Museum...*Berkeley: University of California Press.

Mignot, Claude (1999). *The Pocket Louvre: A Visitor's Guide to 500 Works*. New York: Abbeville Press.

Miltoun, Francis (1910). *Royal Palaces and Parks of France*. L.C. Page & Co.

Nave, Alain (1998). *Treasures of the Louvre*. Barnes & Noble Publishing.

Oliver, Bette Wyn (2007). *From Royal to National: The Louvre Museum and the Bibliothèque Nationale.* Lexington Books.

Tompkins, Calvin (1989). Merchants & Masterpieces: The Story of the Metropolitan Museum of Art. Henry Holt and Company, New York..

Trask, Jeffrey (2012). Things American: Art Museums and Civic Culture in the Progressive Era. University of Pennsylvania Press, Philadelphia.

Free Books by Charles River Editors

We have brand new titles available for free most days of the week. To see which of our titles are currently free, click on this link.

Discounted Books by Charles River Editors

We have titles at a discount price of just 99 cents everyday. To see which of our titles are currently 99 cents, click on this link.

Made in the USA
Middletown, DE
25 July 2021